Single in the Church

Simple Keys to Finding Your Mate

by

Dr. Howard Carter

PublishAmerica
Baltimore

First printing

ISBN: 1-4137-8414-3
PUBLISHED BY PUBLISHAMERICA, LLLP
www.publishamerica.com
Baltimore

Printed in the United States of America

DEDICATION

I'd like to take time to humbly thank my Lord and Savior Jesus Christ. Without HIM I would not have been able to complete this most special work HE Placed in my Heart.

I would also like to thank the four most important women in my life. My grandmother, Mamie King, who has been and continues to be the rock of our family.

Second, I want to thank my mother, Annette Leach, who proved when there is not a man around to help raise the children a strong women of God will always suffice.

Also, I want to thank my aunt, Ennette Leach, who labored alongside my grandmother and mother laying down a godly foundation I would never forget.

Last, but certainly not least, I want to thank my lovely daughter, Cydney. You are truly a blessing and a gift from Almighty God.

I Love you all and thank you so much for all your prayers and support.

ACKNOWLEDGMENTS

This word of praise goes out to all the beautiful ladies who I have had the privilege of knowing. I first want to humbly apologize to each and every one of you for any heartache and pain I may have caused you. Believe me when I tell you I had no idea what wonderful creatures you were, or how much of an impact you could and would have on my life.

Though I was selfish and heartless at times you remained steadfast in your caring and devotion. During the good and the bad times you stood tall and never wavered in your love and support. In spite of my arrogance and conceit you saw a young man full of potential and promise. You sensed a wounded and lame individual, but never gave up for to do that would have been less than honorable. You consistently reached out to help a lost soul, but were more often than not rebuffed. You were ignored and belittled to no end yet you still remained a friend. May GOD bless you with his infinite light of love just for this act alone. Know that your patience and enduring words did not go unheard. Your prayers were not in vain.

Through the grace of the Most High and Awesome GOD, I have been resurrected, redeemed, delivered, and restored. Hallelujah. My eyes have been opened; my heart has been restored; my mind has been renewed; and my life has been saved. I thank each one of you for not giving up on me completely. I know that your prayers were heard. GOD has showed me the error of my ways and has restored my faith. I am comforted knowing why I behaved in the manner in which I did. I realize a life without JESUS is no life at all. It is an empty and barren life destined for condemnation.

That is not the LIFE ordained for me. I am fully aware of this now. All of you ladies out there know who you are. I feel it is vitally important you know you have had a major impact on my life. I draw inspiration from you and that allowed me to write this book.

Having been on both sides of the fence I am acutely aware of the difficulties and loneliness that accompanies a single life. I also know now that it can be overcome if you have a complete understanding of what GOD has planned for your life.

I thank you ALL for your love, patience, kindness, generosity, and prayers. May GOD bless you all.

CONTENTS

PSALM 23

The LORD is my shepherd; I shall not want. He maketh me to lie down in green pastures: he leadeth me beside the still waters. He restoreth my soul: he leadeth me in the paths of righteousness for his name's sake. Yea, though I walk through the valley of the shadow of death, I will fear no evil: for thou art with me; thy rod and thy staff they comfort me. Thou preparest a table before me in the presence of mine enemies: thou anointest my head with oil; my cup runneth over. Surely goodness and mercy shall follow me all the days of my life: and I will dwell in the house of the LORD for ever.

ONE
THE TEMPLE

Know ye Not That Yea Are The Temple Of God,
And That The Spirit Of God Dwelleth In You? (1 Corinthians 3:16)

Women will never be a problem for me, yet women will always be a problem for me.

Someone once uttered these words as he pondered the frustration he encountered each time he sought a wife. It has taken me a few years but I completely understand the internal agony this young man felt. I too feel the exact same way. I can without any conceit or arrogance say that obtaining the companionship of a lady has never been an issue for me. But women are always an issue with me. The difference is I have no problem securing their friendship but somewhere down the line things seem to go awry.

Either I grow discontented with the present relationship or I feel there is some greener grass on the other side of the fence. I have always thought this was some physical and mental mechanism I could fix through my own will. This only led to more frustration and heartbreak and not only for me. There turned out to be one remedy for this habitual problem and his name was Jesus Christ.

The Bible clearly states that the body is the temple of the Holy Ghost and that we are bought with a price and are not our own. We all can attest to that BUT what do you do when you are wrestling with your mind about what your body wants?

Living the single celibate life is one of the most if not the most challenging things for a Christian. Especially when the Christian has already indulged in the sin of premarital sex. There were many Christians who before they gave their life to Christ engaged in this forbidden act of God. But God who is rich in mercy tossed that and every other sin committed into the sea or better yet ocean of forgetfulness. But now that we have been washed in the blood of the Lamb and filled with the Holy Spirit, how do keep from falling back into an act that has been indelibly imprinted in our mind.

For you virgins and who have never engaged in any sexual misconduct, you may not be struggling as those who have already defiled the Temple of God. For you who do fit the aforementioned group who have, this text is especially for you. Nevertheless, virgins please pay attention so you will not find yourself crossing a line that should never be crossed. Let's take a ride down memory lane where all of this began. No I'm not talking about Adam and Eve though that wouldn't be a bad place to start.

IN THE BEGINNING

I'm talking about the day we decided to give up that precious thing called our virginity. When we made this decision outside the confines of the institution of marriage we would have never imagined that one day we would be thrust into spiritual warfare. When most of us made this decision we assumed that from a physical standpoint it was the right thing to do. We wondered why we waited so long for. Most of us were with someone we halfway cared about and honestly thought it could lead to something special.

We found ourselves in the right environment and setting. The lights were dimmed perfectly. Your partner never looked, felt, or smelled better. You had just completed a wonderful evening of dinner and dancing. The atmosphere could not be any better. After deciding whose place would be the scene of the crime you hastened to enter into something so sacred God has forbidden it unless you have been joined together as husband and wife.

Afterwards there is no conviction or condemnation and you decide it felt so wonderful the first time not repeating it over and over and over would be uncivilized. This goes on for many days, weeks, months, and even years until one day God calls you name and commands you to walk in a newness of life you never thought existed.

Now you find yourself part of the Christian family and undergoing the process of sanctification. God is purging you daily and making you more like his Son Jesus. Everyday this change is being produced through the indwelling power of the Holy Spirit.

But there is just one little, tiny, teeny, minuscule, miniature problem. You still have the scars of all your sexual escapades in your mind. You're single, saved, and struggling. Welcome to the club. This is the condition of a great many people in the church family. You art trying desperately to live a life reminiscent of our Savior Jesus Christ while fighting the physical battle of our lives. A war only a Christian can understand.

For though we walk in the flesh, we do not war after the flesh: (For the weapons of our Warfare are not carnal (of the flesh), but mighty through God to the pulling down of Strongholds;) Casting down imaginations (arguments) and every high thing that exalteth Itself against the knowledge of God, and bringing into captivity every though to the Obedience of Christ; And having in a readiness to revenge (punish) all disobedience, When your obedience is fulfilled. (2 Corinthians 10:3-6)

RENEWING THE MIND

Notice the writer of this book is none other than the Apostle Paul. Paul experienced this same battle I am speaking about. Now I am not a theologian but I have taken time to do some studying of the life of the greatest Christian in the history of the world. Now that is a title worth being proud of. However, this same Paul would also pen in the book of Romans chapter seven and verse fourteen, "For We Know That The Law Of God Is Spiritual: But I Am Carnal." I love the way Paul would always say *we know* when discussing the struggles of a Christian's life. Paul would always include himself in the struggles we all have. He had seen things no man had ever seen but he never developed a self-righteous know it all attitude. When Paul's experienced his life changing transformation he would go on to become the greatest missionary the world has or will ever know. In spite of this he readily admitted his struggles and we should thank God he did.

To be single and saved can mean many things. This does not just pertain to the never married men and women who have given their life to Christ, but it includes widows, widowers, and divorced Christians as well. Many people read the book of Corinthians and assume Paul's gift was not being married. I beg to differ. Paul had many gifts but this was not one of them.

Paul was a member of the Sanhedrin council. This is a Jewish sect that would be reminiscent to our Supreme Court. Their platform however was one of a religious nature while the United States Supreme Court focuses on the law. In order for one to be a member of the Sanhedrin he had to be married. So all of you who thought Paul lived a life of celibacy and decided to use this knowledge, as a platform for your celibate life may want to rethink your stand.

Paul states in the book of 1 Corinthians 7:6, "But I speak this by permission and not of commandment." First of all, Paul was responding to a letter sent to him from the Church in Corinth. He lets them know that he is talking to them from his experience and divine revelation. Then he goes on in verse seven and says, "For I would that ALL were even as I myself. But every man hath his proper gift of GOD, one after this manner, and another after that." This verse of scripture has been read and connected to verse 9 which reads, "But if they cannot contain, let them marry for it is better to marry than to burn."

Now reading these two verses would leave one to believe that Paul was indeed an unmarried man whom always lived a celibate life. But, Paul was likely a widowed man who chose not to remarry. Remember

I am not an expert in the life of Paul but my studying leads me to believe Paul had a knowledge regarding certain things that could only come from having been married.

I have never been married so there are many things I can only speculate about through my relationships. However, relationships are quite a distance from actually being married. I may also be able to tap into the knowledge given to me by married couples but these two can never take the place of being thrust into this sacred institution.

I have said all this to say that if the great Apostle Paul himself dealt with lust and temptations it's fair to say we singles today might as well buckle up for the ride. Remember God is no respecter of persons and will not remove any natural desires from your life. Job had his period of trial and tribulation and we shall have ours. However, God never leaves us without ammunition.

Wherefore let him that thinketh he standeth take heed lest he fall. There hath no Temptation overtaken you but such as is common to man: But God is Faithful, who will Not suffer you to be tempted above that ye are able; But will with the temptation also Make a way to escape, that ye may be able to bear (endure) it. (1 Corinthians 10:12-13)

God Resisteth The Proud, But Giveth Grace Unto The Humble. Submit yourselves Therefore to God. Resist the devil, and he will flee from you. (James 4:6-7)

HUMBLE YOURSELF

Understand that all the answers to life's troubles are found in the Word of God. Christians who understand this and learn to stand on the integrity of God's word find dealing with attack much easier. I said it would be easier but it will not be easy. There is a difference between something not being as difficult to deal with and something not being difficult at all. When quoting from Corinthians, I purposely added verse twelve to verse thirteen from First Corinthians chapter ten. I did this to illustrate that you can never allow yourself to get so high-minded, pious, perfunctory, or arrogant that you feel you have the devil whipped.

Never brag in any area you have not been sufficiently tested. When you drop your guard and begin to allow this trap to encase your mind you are headed for a mighty fall. And believe me when you fall you will have a big audience. As long as you are walking circumspectly according to the Word of God and there is not any known or intentional sin in your life it seems as if no one's looking. But if you mess around and slip up, you better believe will find yourself on center stage.

This is why it vitally important that we are cognizant about how we live our everyday lives. Listen my brethren temptation to sin is not sin. And the closer you get to God the stronger the temptations will be. But be not alarmed God has said he will never leave us nor forsake us and I love him just enough to believe HIM. I sincerely hope you do too.

The Bible says we are "a living epistle" and it is never more evident than when a brother or sister in the church family falls into sexual sin. Notice when you fall your title comes into play. You start hearing I can't believe Deacon hotshot cheated. Can you believe Elder Know It All was caught with her? Did you hear what happened to Minister Never Lie? Before the fall you were brother or sister but now your title is magnified.

Now we all know no one is immune to temptation and we are actually exhorted to expect it each and every day. But what you will find is the more you attend church, pray, and read your bible the more intense the struggles will become. I'll prove it to you.

The Bible says in the gospel of Matthew and the fourth chapter that once baptized by John the Baptist, our LORD and Savior Jesus Christ was led (Mark's Gospel says he was driven) by the Spirit into the wilderness to be tempted of the devil. Here Jesus has just had the Spirit descending like a dove, and lighting upon him. He hasn't preached one sermon and God makes a powerful statement and says, "This is my beloved Son, in whom I am well pleased."

Who's the next joker Jesus sees? You've got it. That same liar from the Genesis chapter three. Jesus didn't get a pulpit he got the father of lies. Jesus didn't receive a budget or a preaching itinerary. He was given the opportunity to look the enemy right square in the face. Now what did Jesus have to fight with? The very same thing we have. The pure unadulterated, immutable, incomparable Word of God. Jesus quoted scripture three times when confronted about something he knew was against the will of God.

Like Jesus, God has an earthly destiny for our lives and the devil and his henchmen have one goal and purpose in mind. That is to kill, steal, and destroy you and the plan God has for you. And they will do any and everything possible to systematically tear you down. The battle may be a series of little wars with the goal being to leave you utterly destroyed and God looking like a fool.

But know the Bible says, "Greater is he that is in you than he that is in the world." This is truth that has to stick with you forever. James 1:21 states, "The Engrafted Word of God Is Able to Save Your Souls." Webster's dictionary shows one definition of graft as a transplanting of skin. This means the Word of God has to be transplanted to your heart and mind.

The devil will always attempt to destroy you by trying to use any thing that he knows

is diametrically opposed to the Word of God. Now if you do not have this Word transplanted you will not be able to use it when needed. If your mind is being deluged by the demonic presence of Satan and his lying bandits scripture must be readily available. When demonic spirits try and emit havoc in your mind you may not have time to run and get your Bible.

Therefore, what you know will become vitally important. Daniel 11:32 says, "...the people that do know their God shall be strong, and do exploits." If you don't know God then taking action against Satan will not be possible. You heard from the Word and not just my mouth. There is scripture in the Bible to deal with any issue life might present. It is up to us to diligently read and study so we are equipped when needed.

LAW IS LIGHT

Many people think that Jesus came to abolish the Law of God, but that couldn't be further from the truth. The Bible tell us that God's new covenant would call for Christians to not have to look at two tablets in order to know what God expected, but that the law would be inscribed internally. Note the following scripture written by Apostle Paul.

Ye are our epistle written in our hearts, known and read of ALL men: Forasmuch as ye Are manifestly declared to be the epistle of Christ ministered by us written not with ink, But with the Spirit of the living God; not in tables (tablets) of stone, but in FLESHY Tables (tablets) of the HEART. (2 Corinthians 3:2-3)

Let's look at the capped words. We are God's living epistles that will be read by ALL men. You read this and get an understanding of why Paul exhorted us to present our bodies a living sacrifice. Until you completely submit yourself to God you are open to fall into the trap of any of Satan's schemes. If you become the unfortunate victim of the devil you will now be on public display. When you read the Bible you notice that many might men of God fell because of sexual sin. And when they fell it never was a secret affair.

We must understand that when we profess to be Christians we immediately become targets and our name go up on the betting board. Once this happens people begin taking bets on when and how we will fall. I have found out that people I thought cared about me were the very people who bet against me. They considered my new life a charade and bet I wouldn't last longer than a J-Lo marriage.

I am telling you that there will always be odds being laid on your life. And there will be waiting and hoping for you to fall. Therefore, it is imperative you get into the Word of God and get the Word of God into you. It will not happen through osmosis. I'm sorry to be the one to tell you this but you are going to have to knock the dust off the Bible, cut the television off, get somewhere quiet and spend time reading God's word. The Word of God is your sword against the enemy.

Know this for a surety the world will think you are off you rocker when you take a stand for holiness and purity. They will think you have been using some new and improved drug when you talk about abstinence until marriage. They will ridicule you and talk about you but please think it not strange because this is a sure fire indication you are right where God would have you to be. When you are out-of-step with the world you we be in-step with God.

I recall a time I was reading the Sunday morning newspaper and happen to notice an article involving Miss America 2003. She was planning a campaign for youth in America. Part of her campaign encompassed her speaking to youth about remaining abstinent until marriage.

The pageant officials were actually trying to bully this woman into refraining from speaking on this topic. After two days of discussion she prevailed. But do you see how the world views holiness and purity. It is something their natural minds just cannot comprehend. To think adults whether they be Christians or not would have reservation about someone teaching the principle of not having sex until marriage.

Beloved, please do not be surprised at the persecution you will endure to live a righteous and holy life.

The last two capped words go together. FLESHY HEART. This is the location in which the Word of God must be written. You must understand that Jesus didn't come to abolish the Law of God but he came to change the location. Rather than on tablets of stone it would now be on your heart. Rather than being held bondage by the letter of the law we would surrender ourselves to the spirit of the law.

This is what allows you to find a way of escape. In the Book of Genesis there is a story in chapter thirty-nine which gives an account of Joseph and Potiphar's wife. Potiphar was an officer of Pharaoh, the Egyptian king. Joseph had just been bought and given a position in the house of Potiphar.

The Bible says in verse two the LORD was with Joseph, and he was a prosperous (successful) man and he was in the house of his Egyptian master. It is so much in that I could stay there for days. I'll make a few points and move on.

First, God never sees situations we are in the way we see them. Joseph has been bought as a slave, yet God says he was a prosperous and successful man. He's a slave at this point of his life but God doesn't see the bondage the way Joseph does. God will put you in tight situations to increase maturity. Therefore, never complain when you are in the jail that leads to your promise.

Second, he is put into a house and that was undoubtedly better than a field so God was truly with him in this aspect or so it would seem. My main point comes regarding what happens while he is in the house. Potiphar's wife finds Joseph irresistible and launches a no holds barred attack to get Joseph to engage in a sexual tryst. Sexual temptation has found it's way at door of the Man of God and I just pointed out to you that the LORD was with him.

So how was Joseph able to rebuff her advances? In verse nine of that same chapter Joseph gives the reason every Christian must have etched into his or her heart when tempted to sin. Let's take a gander at what Joseph said to the enemy in verse nine of chapter thirty-nine of the Book of Genesis. He said, "there is none greater in this house than I; neither hath he kept back any thing from me but thee (wife), because thou art his wife: how then can I DO THIS GREAT WICKEDNESS, AND SIN AGAINST GOD?"

That's how you defeat the enemy when he mounts up an attack against you. When you

find yourself in this situation speak what you know. You submit yourself to God and His Word. You must remember that the Ten Commandments of God were given to Moses over in the next chapter so where was this sin written for Joseph know it.

Do I dare say it was written on the fleshy part of his precious heart? Understand something, when we are born into this world we are born natural liars. If a little boy or girl does something there parent tells them not to do instead of telling the truth they are lie. Now I've heard preaching regarding this side many times, but have you ever wondered why they lied?

Could it be possible that somewhere on their little hearts, God's law has been written? Then why tell the lie? The truth always bares consequences many people cannot handle. This is why if you ever purpose in your heart to live your life according to the Truth, which is the Word of God, there will be consequences that will leave you alone and wondering.

Wondering if choosing God was the right thing to do. You may think it won't happen but there will be times when you are going to wish you could do some of the things you used to do. This happens to all of us some time or another so please do not feel bad.

RESIST THE ENEMY

Now notice whom Joseph says he would be sinning against if he did the wicked deed. He didn't view the sin as a breach against Potiphar or his wife. Even though Potiphar had given him Carte' blanche in the entire house he still considered God as chief authority of his life. In spite of all this earthly power, Joseph felt if he allowed himself to be pulled into this sexual sin, it would be a great sin against God. You will also notice I called Potiphar's wife the enemy. Well beloved hear this, any person, place, or thing that attempts to disconnect you from God and his purpose and destiny for your life is not a friend.

I would suggest if you haven't read the entire account of Joseph you should make it your business to do just that. If it means putting this book down right now I beseech you to do it if so led. Please remember that any written work by any man can never hold a candle to God's Word.

You will see that there was a plan and purpose for Joseph's life right from the beginning. Now Joseph saw all the positives of his destiny in his dreams but never saw the pit or the jail. He only saw the palace and that happens in our lives. We see the blessings but never the problems. But just think for a moment what would have happen if Joseph would have given in to the sexual advances of Potiphar's wife. That would have been the blow that the devil was hoping for.

Now it would not have completely thwarted God's plan but Joseph's life. But it could have disqualified him from being a part of God's providential plan to relieve Jacob and his family from famine. If because of your disobedience you become disqualified from a promise, God will still see his plan through. God is never caught off guard when we fail in life.

Samson would also come up against temptation from a woman. However, the story would end totally different. I will not insult your intelligence by recanting this story but note how two men of God both endured temptation and yet the outcomes were totally different. The outcome for the enemy was the same because the enemy will always be defeated. But God's outcome for the men was to be the same. God's expected end is always one filled with prosperity and peace. So when you come up against temptation you must ask yourself one question.

Do I want to be a Joseph or a Samson?

Listen it does not matter who you are or what title you hold, you can rest assure that you will be tempted by the devil. Let me go a step further and say you may even find yourself doing the tempting. I have had female ministers, elders, ushers, choir members, parishioners, and even pastors make sexual advances toward me. You want more? I have even had male Christians who have not been delivered from homosexuality make sexual advances towards me. Close your mouth. I have gotten to the point in my life where nothing people do ever surprises me. This is why you must be armed with the Word of God.

Not only must we be armed with the Word we must pray continuously that God fills our spirit man. We should also make an effort to intercede in prayer for the entire body of Christ. It doesn't help the body when instead of praying for one another we spread gossip. This is just as bad as sexual sin because it cuts at the moral fiber of an individual. People can get over the act of a sexual interlude easier than they can get over having their name scandalized regarding the same sexual act.

When a person falls into sexual sin and repents to God it becomes an issue between the sinner and God. But when everybody in the church knows about the sin because of gossip, it can become difficult for the sinner to show his or her face in God's house. The problem with this is if we sin the place should be able to come and feel comforted should be the church. I am not against the leadership of the church dealing with the sinner to ensure it doesn't become a habitual problem. As long as we do it in the spirit of meekness and kindness there should be no problem for any of the parties involved. Coming to God and God's family should always bring a sense of peace to a sinner's life. Therefore, run to God when trouble occurs and not from God.

Unfortunately, many church members especially those in positions of leadership are exhibiting more carnal behavior than many of the members. This is proving to be disturbing because so many Christians assume that the ministers, deacons, ushers, and pastors are in possession of some different Holy Spirit than they are. Not So.

They must pray and seek God just as much if not more to fend off the demonic attacks of the enemy. I know a few too many people in leadership who because of a weak prayer and study life succumb to fornication, self-gratification, and even adultery. And yes masturbation is sin. How? I'm glad you asked.

Masturbation violates the number seventh and tenth commandment of God. The number seven commandment says, "Thou shalt not commit adultery." The tenth commandment says, "Thou shalt not covet thy neighbor's house, thou shalt not coveth thy neighbor's wife, nor his manservant, nor his maidservant, nor his ox, nor his ass, nor any thing that is his neighbor's."

EQUALLY INCLUSIVE

First of all understand that fornication relates to all acts of sexual immorality. It doesn't only relate to actual sexual intercourse. Second, masturbation requires you to take your mind off God and put it somewhere else. You have to focus on something or someone and here is covetousness, which is idolatry. This is very serious in the eyes of God. Do not think this is a convenient way to relieve one's self while remaining celibate. ALL sexual immorality is sin.

Remember Jesus introduced us to the Spirit of the Law by explaining if a man looked upon a woman with lust in his HEART he has already committed adultery. Jesus says that the only thing that prevented the act was that there was no opportunity. Remove that element and the man commits the act. Saints of God we must understand the seriousness of not remaining pure while unmarried. The best ways for Satan to derail a single Christian is to destroy his reputation and character by inducing him/her into habitual sexual sin.

I started this chapter talking about keeping the temple (which is your body) pure. We also should be careful not to yield our members to anything ungodly. Anything that we could do that would put us in direct conflict with God is something we should not yield to. There are some issues many of us have regarding the ability or willingness to commit. I call it commitment phobia. Many people have no problem committing, but seem to go from one bad relationship to another.

Regardless of your situation we all must know how to yield to the power of the Holy Spirit. This is key if we are ever going to rid ourselves of these evil problems. If we do not gain control over these behaviors, singleness and frustration will be the order of the day. It would be downright tragic to live a life single when God had a person prepared and waiting just for you.

Therefore, we must do everything to avoid terminating the union plans God wants us to enjoy. If you have a problem committing to a man or woman you should realize that you have help in the name of Jesus. There is no need for you to miss out on the promises God has for your life. Just seek him regarding this weak area and he will see you through. You have now had your excuse removed regarding your plight. Just remember patience will be a virtue in allowing God to do his mighty work in your life.

If commitment is truly your issue you must allow yourself to grow in stages. Just because you are a Christian you cannot immediately seek marriage. Let God help you develop the strength to maintain a healthy platonic friendship before moving on to a relationship. Once you have established yourself at that stage then move to the stage of a non-sexual monogamous union. This should place you in a much better position for marriage. Single and saved is never a reason to rush to the altar. Praying daily and communicating with your newly found friend can also be the spiritual medicine you need.

If you have a problem maintaining a relationship you should seek

God in prayer to find out what you an individual may be doing wrong. If your relationships start off well and die out at the hint of marriage, you need to seek God to stem the tide in this area. If you have desires of getting married and your partner does not this should definitely be taken to the LORD in prayer. You are obviously choosing people who are not compatible for you. Discernment in this area will be crucial if heartache is to be prevented.

Christians should be seeking to marry with the purpose of a continued life of dating. Contrary to what the world does we should not be dating to marry. The longest chapter in the book of Genesis (chapter twenty-four) concentrated on the sole subject of marriage. God feels so strong about marriage he took the longest chapter in the first book of his Word to show us how we should find a mate.

God gives us a view of how we should allow the Holy Spirit to be our guide in finding and choosing a mate. We too often allow external circumstances to become the overriding factor in finding a mate. This is contrary to how God would have us do things. This reluctance to yield to a higher power is what causes many of our fleshy problems. Nevertheless, we must always be mindful of our bodies now that we belong to God. A heavy price was paid for our freedom and we should never forget it.

I do understand that this can be easier said than done. The apostle Paul gave us a panoramic view of what it is like to have the inner struggle of two natures. He explains in detail that the law of God is perfect and it is the flesh nature of man that proves to be no good. When I speak of the flesh I am not actually talking about the physical body, but the condition of being dominated by sin and sinful pursuits.

FLESH AND SPIRIT

I want to take the time and compare scripture to our personal lives. The text comes from the book of Romans and chapter number seven. In verse number fourteen Paul says, "The law is spiritual: but I am carnal, sold under sin." We see here that God's law is consistent with the nature of God. Our God is perfect, holy, divine, and pure. We on the other hand are imperfect, greedy, selfish, hateful, prideful, and arrogant.

He expounds on the fact that the very things he wants to do he does not do and the very things he does not want to do he does. He has to agree that when he transgresses the law that the law is good and his flesh is not. He also understands that when he sins living holy is the right thing to do. He would have never known how good it is to live right without the benefit of the law. He expounds in verse eighteen that "in his flesh dwelleth no good thing: for to will is present with me; but how to perform that which is good I find not." I wanted you to read it hear but take a moment and find it in your Bible.

When you read this you begin to feel the pain of apostle Paul was feeling. He concludes that in his flesh nature nothing good can be produced. In his mind he wants to do right but he doesn't know how. He finally has to ask who can deliver this wretched man from this body of death. I am sure many of you don't know what that is all about because of your perceived holiness and righteousness. But for the rest of who know what it is like to struggle with our flesh, remember we have reason to have hope.

I know Christians who love Jesus with all of their heart. These are Christians who know they have had a one on experience with the LORD. They were smoking the joint and the spirit of God took over and they put it down and vowed to never go back. I know men who got out the bed from a night of copulation and cried for God to help them and he did. There are women who compromised themselves and vowed it was the last time and proceeded to throw away their lover's key. I know people who put the liquor bottle down and walked away with the intention of never coming back.

I am talking about people who have had a Damascus road experience with the LORD only to find themselves living right here in Romans chapter seven. Their minds do not want any part of the past life or past experiences. They want to live right for Jesus. They want God to use them in a mighty way. There are dreams and visions of a better future for them and their families. They proceed to begin this arduous journey of walking with God.

Then all of a sudden temptation comes and in a moment and a twinkling of an eye a pothole knocks them off track. He is back in the bed with Sally, she is on the couch with Butch, he is smoking again with the fellows, and they are waking up in a drunken stupor.

Inebriated, they all grapple to figure out how they ended up in a place they vowed they would never see again. The sad part about this is that it doesn't happen just once but several times. These folks even begin to question whether or not they are really saved. My answer to that is if you are concerned then you don't have to worry about your salvation.

You are experiencing the convicting power that the Holy Spirit brings. You are grieving the daylights out of the Holy Spirit but you are not a lost cause. Psalm 37:23-24 says, "The steps of a good or righteous man are ordered by the LORD: and he delighteth in his way. Though he fall, he shall not be utterly cast down: for the LORD upholdeth him with his hand."

Scripture says you will fall. Notice the text says, "though he fall" as to say you will not see all the potholes and will occasionally fall. But God never leaves you or releases your hand once you belong to him. What a reassuring feeling it is to know God always has our hands. He goes on to say he will uphold you with his hand. When you find yourself somewhere doing something with someone you never envisioned always learn from that mistake. You may want to retrace your steps to find out how you ended up sleeping with her or him, smoking whatever it is you smoke, or drinking whatever it is you drink.

This is the part you must play in order to spiritually grow and to not continue walking in a life of sin. The Bible says, "Greater is he that is in you than he that is in the world." You have power to defeat sin now that you are saved. You don't have to give in to these temptations. The temptations are evident now because of the Holy Spirit's presence. When you experienced temptation prior to being saved it wasn't even temptation because you didn't have to be tempted to do any of those things.

It is the presence of the Holy Spirit that gives you the signal there is something wrong and potential sin is in the midst. Prior to your conversion you would not have only been ready, willing, and able but you would have been a recruiter for the devil. You would eagerly search to find others who wanted to participate in your sinful escapades. But 2 Corinthians 5:17 says, "…if any man be in Christ, he is a new creation: old things are passed away; behold all things are become new." The old is passed away and you are a new man or woman. You are not held hostage by sin anymore. There will always be a way of escape from any sinful situation you may find yourself in. One of the most important things God says in his Word is that we are not ignorant of Satan's devices or schemes. This is important because since we are not ignorant and we now have power we should not be defeated.

If a baseball player is at the plate waiting for the pitcher to throw the ball he will stand a better chance at hitting a home run if he knows what the pitch will be. By the same token if the pitcher can throw a pitch the batter is not expecting he can strike him out. The battle inside our temple becomes a winning battle when we know Satan's schemes. This begins with knowing our weaknesses.

He will prey on the very thing that easily besets us. If you don't have a desire for cocaine you can best believe Satan will not be tempting you in that area. If the lust for men or women is not your vice you won't have to worry about him launching an attack there. If you can be around alcohol and it doesn't bother you then that is not where the assault will come from.

Whatever you are finding as an individual vice or struggle, you can bet the farm he will be attacking you right there. That is why God says we are not ignorant of his devices. I've said on many occasions that Satan can be called many things but lazy is not one of them. He is always busy accusing, lying, cheating, and tempting the brethren. He hates you and me because we are the apples of God's eye. He is constantly trying to short-circuit the plan God has for our lives. He hates the fact we took his job of praise and worship and will never let us rest. He will pull out all the stops to ensure disaster for every Christian.

He is cunning and crafty and will use our own weakness against us if we allow it. Therefore, your quest to defeat Satan begins and ends with you. How do you build up your defense? I'm glad you asked. Let's run over to the book of Ephesians chapter number six and see what God says.

ARMOR OF GOD

Always refer to the Bible when needed to find an answer to life's difficulties. Christians need not seek soothsayers, witches, or self-help gurus to ascertain what the will for their life is. God has the answers before Satan can form the question out of his lying mouth. I want you to memorize these verses and get them in your mind and heart. These verses could possibly save your life one day.

Be strong in the LORD, and in the power of his might. Put on the whole armor of God, That ye may be able to stand against the wiles (schemes) of the devil. For we wrestle Not against flesh and blood, but against principalities, against powers, against the rulers Of the darkness of this world, against spiritual wickedness in high places. Wherefore, Take unto you the whole armor of God, that ye may be able to withstand in the evil Day, and having done all, to stand. Stand therefore, having your loins girt about with Truth, and having on the breastplate of righteousness, and your feet shod with the Preparation of the gospel of peace; above all, taking the shield of faith, wherewith ye Shall be able to quench all the fiery darts of the wicked. And take the helmet of Salvation, and the sword of the Spirit, which is the Word of God. Praying always with All prayer and supplication in the Spirit and watching thereunto with all perseverance And supplication for all saints.
(Ephesians 6:10-18)

So we see we are to be strong in the LORD and not ourselves. The whole armor of God is comprised of six pieces. The first is Truth that comes from knowing the Word of God. Second, is the Breastplate of Righteousness that represents a holy character and moral conduct derived from the first piece. The third piece is Preparation of Peace that is the eagerness to put the Truth into action. The fourth piece is the Shield of Faith that is the belief in the Truth of God's Word. The fifth piece is the Helmet of Salvation that comes from the assurance of salvation and deliverance. The sixth and final piece is the Sword of the Spirit, which is the Word of God.

The entire counsel of the Bible and not just a few scriptures sought on daily basis. In other words, read the entire book. If someone gave you this book to read I would hope you would begin from the beginning. If that is what you would do in this case then that is where you should begin reading the Bible as well.

Now after you have put on all six pieces be diligent in developing your prayer life. You should pray without ceasing meaning you should be constantly speaking with God. Finally, we are to watch out for our fellow Christian brethren. We should pray not only that we be delivered from evil but that God would deliver our neighbors as well.

MASS AFFECT

Some of you may not believe it but personal sin affects everybody. Proverbs 14:34 says, "Righteousness exalteth a nation: but sin is a reproach (shame or disgrace) to any people." This means when you are in the confines of your home and think your sin is only affecting you think again. When you see the homosexual and lesbian community parading their sinful behavior in the face of the nation do you think it is only affecting them?

Children are watching and their minds are fertile soil to every seed that is planted. And if I may say, it is not only children but also weak-minded adults who feel if others sin is permissible then why shouldn't mind be. We watch married athletes being accused of rape and what do we say? We say please don't let him be convicted of rape because she had have consented.

We totally forget that though he may be innocent of rape he still admitted he committed adultery. What we are saying is rape is not acceptable but we'll wink at adultery. This is why God must and will judge the sin of man. We won't judge it correctly so we leave it to God to administer the punishment. It is so in the life of the individual and in the life of the nation.

We use a double standard to deal with moral wrong. We say to the world you can police this sin over here but don't touch this over there. Why? Because it leaves something for us to fall into without be ridiculed and ostracized. If we condemn both then we are forced to live our lives in a holy fashion. If we start yelling from the rooftops that rape and adultery are equally bad in the eyes of God, we now have to be careful we never fall into the lesser of the world's two.

The church has on more than one occasion proven we will jump headfirst into adultery just a quick as the heathen. So what we do is simply turn a blind eye and then expect God to reward us for a job well done. The church had better grow up and do it fast because Jesus is coming back. We are so petrified of the thought of living holy we leave wiggle room by the mere act of remaining quiet. When righteous people do nothing the wicked will always win. We shriek at the thought of someone digging into our lives. We shudder at the thought of something being found.

The last thing we want is someone bringing up our latest transgression. So rather than seeking holiness we will give certain immoral behavior two thumbs up as long as it doesn't affect our home. Rather than rock the boat of the community we just go on living our little Christian lives as if we are part of a private club. God didn't save us to form a private club. He saved us that we might go out and be disciples for others. This is why we must pray for our neighbors as well as ourselves. Proverbs 24:17 says, "Rejoice NOT when thine enemy falleth, and let not thine heart be glad when he stumbleth."

Christians should never be happy at the demise of wickedness of any person. We should become intercessors and seek the same Grace and Mercy for their lives as God showed on our lives.

We must also understand that before God destroyed Sodom and Gomorrah the great patriarch Abraham did something we should all learn from. Abraham began a bargaining session with God relating to the destroying of the land if righteous were with the unrighteous. He started with fifty and worked his way down by to ten to ten. Abraham did this to save his nephew Lot and his family. Though Sodom and Gomorrah was a sin-infested land Abraham knew a godly man was there and needed to be saved.

This is the perfect example of God's grace and mercy. But it could not have come if Abraham did not step in. The world we live in would put Sodom and Gomorrah to shame and if God does not destroy this world in the same fashion he owes Sodom and Gomorrah an apology. This is why sin must be eradicated and it starts with one individual at a time.

SELF CLEANSING

Cleanse your temple of all filthiness of the spirit and flesh while perfecting holiness unto God. This is our reasonable service now that we are God's children. We are to submit ourselves to the power of the spirit in all manners of life. There is a term in basketball called "short clocked" and it refers to a team taking too long to get into place to run a play. The reason is because of the pressure being applied by the defense.

When Satan applies pressure and we succumb we get "short clocked" and thereby have less time to do what God wants us to do. And if the clock expires before the offense gets off a shot they lose possession of the ball. When we miss what God has for us because of our inability to get past the pressure applied in life we lose possession of what God had for us.

This is one of the things God means when he says, "the wealth of the sinner is laid up for the righteous." It is laid up because we cannot or will not defeat this sin mentality. Wealth is not only money, but is about the blessings God has for his people. The Bible says in Jeremiah that in righteousness we shall be established and in the book of Job he says when we decree or say a thing it shall be established.

When you put these two together it gives a perfect view of how the Christian will be able to receive the things God has for him. He must establish a holy life that has been purchased for him through the blood of Jesus. He then must pray and seek God's will for his life. When the Christian experiences these two he then can decree anything according to God's will and it shall come to pass.

I cannot fully delineate the importance holy living is to God. This is his standard and it is the foundation of our salvation. We are saved by grace and through faith but it was the works of a holy lived by Jesus that proved pleasing to God. It was also this holy life that gave us the righteous standing we now possess.

Jesus didn't sin once from the time he came out of Mary's womb to the time he uttered those immortal words, "It is finished." He was completely blameless, sinless, and without reproach. There was no guile in his mouth and no one could find any fault in him. It was works that saved us, but not our works. It was the beginning and the finished work of Jesus Christ.

God now expects us to strive for that same holiness in appreciation for the free gift of salvation. We may fall short but it should not be for lack of trying. The difference between people who have had a one on one experience with Jesus and those who think it is cool to profess Christianity comes down to one thing. When Christians who truly love the LORD sin they simply hate it. They can't stand the fact they can't get over whatever it is they are struggling with. They vow to whip it and seek any way to do just that. They exude zeal and fortitude to want to please God and not continue to be viewed as weak.

Those who simply profess Christianity could care less when they sin. They sleep around with any Tom, Dick or Harry and never feel any remorse whatsoever. The get high on drugs and alcohol and never lose a moment of sleep about it. They sleep with every Sally, Sue, and Jane they can find and never wish they felt different about it. These are the people who Jesus says he will one day judge and decree I never knew you so depart from me. It is serious business to call oneself a Christian. You are saying you represent God's only begotten Son and that is serious business my friend.

Something we should know as we deal with sin is if we are willing to tolerate it, we will never change it. The Bible says in 2 Peter 1:20-21, "Knowing this first, that no prophecy of the scripture is of an private interpretation or origin. For the prophecy came not in old (any) time by the will of man: but holy men of God spake as they were moved by the Holy Ghost (Spirit)."

Great stuff but notice God says holy men spoke. Now you tell me what was holy about Peter? He denied the LORD three times and was known to give you a good cussing if necessary. What was holy about Paul? He persecuted Christians to no end and even conspired to the murder of many of them. What was holy about Solomon? He was a womanizer and a polygamist?

What was holy about Moses? He disobeyed God to the point he wasn't even allowed to walk on the land that was promised. John Mark who wrote the Gospel of St. Mark walked out on the greatest missionary team in world history (Paul and Barnabas). Where was Matthew during the crucifixion? He wasn't at the foot of the cross. But God says holy men wrote.

These men started out one way but through the power of the Holy Spirit there lives were changed in a way never known to modern man. They went from being cowards to courageous in one night. They turned from persecuting Christians to preaching Christ in one fell swoop. They realized that all the womanizing and money was pure vanity without the presence of God. They regained the vigor to run the race and became titans in the faith.

God always sees you in victory. He can see you overcoming that sin nature and winning the battle. He called Gideon a mighty man a valor when he was living a cowardice life. He called David (The Eventual King of Israel) a "Man after my heart" while David was keeping sheep.

Our God always sees us in a light much different than the light we see ourselves. But beloved, it doesn't have to remain that way. We can begin to see ourselves different if we allow Jesus to not only be Savior but LORD. I envisioned this very book being written and published over two years ago. It didn't come to fruition at that time but I saw it happen in my Spirit. It took some time for it to be manifested but low and behold you are reading it. Hallelujah.

Therefore, you must understand I am not writing to
you about something I read or heard preached. I am a living witness

and miracle that if God said it, let HIM be true and every man and devil who contradicts HIM be a liar. Your temple is such a prized possession that there are no words that could truly convey it. If it were not do you think the enemy would be doing everything it could to destroy it.

Anything that the enemy tries to destroy must be a threat or it would be a waste of time to destroy it. We are so special to God. He loves us and wants us to live life in the fullness of victory and joy. We can and we will but it must begin with us. This is why I put this chapter first because if we miss this chapter the rest of the book and our lives will mean absolutely nothing. We will always be struggling Christians while awaiting heaven.

Song of Solomon 2:7 says, "I charge you (adjure you), O ye daughters of Jerusalem, by the roes, and by the hinds (gazing through) of the field, that ye stir not up, nor awake my love, till he please." God is saying that we should refrain from arousing any sexual desire before it is time. Refrain means to desist, abstain, hold back, forbear, forgo, do without, avoid, eschew, cease, stop, give up, leave off, quit, renounce, rebuke, rebuff, and any other words you may know which may apply. We are charged to do it.

God says we have power that allows us to do it so we must do it. He is not going to do it for us. We may be in the midst of our toughest fight but we must refrain. We may be in the middle of our biggest temptation, but we must refrain. We may feel all hell is about to break loose around our entire life but we must refrain. We must refrain I tell you because our integrity is on the line. If you need more motivation to refrain take a look at the last three words of the scripture. It says, "Till he please."

You see there is a proper time for our desires to be fed and I will delve into that more in the coming chapters but God has said he would not leave us comfortless. This is a promise he meant in more ways than one. Understand this, there are more things in the atonement than you think. Hebrews 6:9 says, "…beloved, we are persuaded (confident of) better things (concerning) of you, and things that ACCOMPANY salvation." Verse ten says, "God is not unrighteous to forget YOUR WORK and LABOR of LOVE, which ye have showed toward his name."

This is why preaching the gospel the way Jesus, John the Baptist, Paul, and Peter did will prove to be quite sufficient. Every ministry in this world that professes Jesus as the Christ should be majoring on the all-sufficient work of Christ, our justification by the imputation of his righteousness, and our acceptance in union with him.

The forming of individual ministries focusing on one thing is *nothing*. What good does it do to heal a man, put money in the pockets of a man, try and deliver a man from the world's diseases or increase a man's faith if that man has not a saving knowledge of our LORD Jesus Christ?

Get that same man to receive Christ in his heart and watch the Holy Spirit give that man peace to deal with any ill. Watch that man with zeal strive to obtain wealth that he may further the gospel of Jesus Christ. Watch that man be delivered from every wicked and evil tool the devil has.

And watch that man through biblical study and prayer increase in faith and love. Healing is in the atonement. Financial prosperity is in the atonement. Deliverance from sin is in the atonement. Faith is in the atonement. Everything we are ever going to need is in the atonement.

NEVER SATISFIED

I started this chapter talking about the dilemma I found myself in when I would be dating one person and seeing something better. Know of a surety this is a trick that Satan has been using for thousands of years. Do not for one moment think you are immune to this happening. You may find yourself in a union that may seem to be a gift from God himself. Be very careful.

Everything that glitters is not gold and looks can truly be deceptive. In the very first book of the Bible the devil used this subtle move of deception to separate Abraham and Lot. Both men were blessed of God with many possessions of flocks, herds, and tents. This in the modern day would be translated cars, houses, and money.

They had so much that there was not enough land for both men to dwell. At least this was the trick propagated by Satan. There was strife between the herdsmen of Abraham and Lot as a result of all this. Genesis 13:10 says, "And Lot lifted up his eyes and beheld all the plain of Jordan, that it was well watered every where, before the LORD destroyed Sodom and Gomorrah, even as the garden of the LORD, like the land of Egypt, as thou comest unto Zoar. Then Lot chose him all the plain of Jordan."

The land Lot chose would eventually be overrun with so much homosexuality and perversion, God destroyed it with fire and brimstone.

The land was excellent land for livestock according to the naked eye. However, lying beneath that posh exterior was such evil and wickedness had Abraham not prayed to God, Lot and his entire family would have been destroyed. The grass was definitely not greener on the other side.

It is the same today whether we are talking about land or people. The temple is something we must always cherish. We cannot allow our eyes to sign checks our bodies may have to cash. Therefore, remember we are not our own any more and as we continue growing it is the blood of Christ that paid the price we could never pay.

So we should glorify God with our bodies until he connects us with our mate. He'll do it but remember he who is faithful in a few things will be rulers over much and to much is given much is required. We must show faithfulness in our singleness if we are to receive the blessings God wants us to have.

DON'T LOWER THE STANDARDS

I hate to go off on a tangent but I must. I was talking to a young lady one day and she said some things that simply threw me for a loop. While discussing the possibility of beginning a relationship she expressed concerns regarding why it wouldn't be a good idea for her. She felt that a long-distance relationship would be more than she could handle. I could understand this but then the conversation really became interesting.

She went on to say although she was raised in a church I seemed too religious for her. She finished explaining he position by concluding that I seemed to have a lot going for me and that she was sure I would find someone special.

Now wasn't that really sweet of her to say. I am being as sarcastic as I possibly can without cussing. Not because I am upset it didn't work out but because of the stance this kind of attitude portrays.

This was coming from an educated, attractive, gainfully employed, and supposedly Christian woman. If this is the type of utter nonsense that is coming from Christian women's mouths it's a wonder our relationships are going to hell.

Let's dissect what this woman told me. First of all she expressed concerns with the distance. Men and women of God if you are truly expecting love do not box yourself in by limiting yourself to a few miles. You would be doing such a disservice to yourself. How can you make a conscious decision to eliminate everyone who does not live in a twenty-mile radius? We have cars, buses, trains, and planes to transport us from one place to another. What this also suggests is that if you happen to take a trip anywhere all potential suitors at that location can simply forget it.

This is why God says his thoughts and our thoughts are different. We confine God's ability to help us find someone because we have boxed him into a few miles. Let's not allow small-mindedness to shorten our dating pool.

The second excuse was the one that completely blew my mind. She felt I was too religious. The first thing I want to explain is that being spiritual and being religious is not the same. Spiritual and religion are not synonyms. Religion is man trying to reach God while spirituality represents man accepting what God did for him at the cross.

Nevertheless, to hear this from any Christian is cause for concern. It is usually their way of saying they don't live their life completely for God. However, when a woman makes a statement like this it is cause for even more concern. Women in my opinion are the key to the dating process in the Christian circle so I was very concerned.

I was concerned because I want to know why a woman wouldn't want a man who loved Jesus? If she felt I loved Jesus to the point it exuded in everything I said or did, how could she deem this to be a negative? In this day and age how could a Christian women find fault in this quality? The ultimate act of commitment a man could ever make is to give his life to the LORD. If a man can commit to a God whom he cannot see how much more faithful would he be if he committed to a woman whom he can see? Ladies please wake up.

The third thing she said which wasn't an excuse but made her entire position more ridiculous was that she felt I had a lot going for me and I would make someone a perfect mate. Now remember we were mutually attracted to one another before she this barrage of excuses. My question here is why couldn't I make her a perfect mate?

Some will say she said those things because she didn't want to hurt my feelings. Well I would never give anyone an appearance of ignorance and unfaithfulness to God so I wouldn't hurt someone's feelings. If we cannot be truthful in the embryo stages of the relationship then when can we be?

The beginning is the best time to be truthful. There are no emotional ties so if the relationship doesn't work out neither party has invested any major time or treasure. Moreover, we are Christians and our lives should reflect such. I would rather hear constructive criticism that I can grow from than to hear a lie just to appease my feelings. I sincerely hope I received a few *Amens* from that statement.

The reason I decided to write about this personal experience is because this type of ridiculous fodder women and sometimes men spew causes everyone to lose. Christian woman all over the country are narrowing the standards so much that it doesn't take anything for a guy today to gain access to her body or mind.

The men today feel like they don't have to buy flowers. They don't have to buy candy. They don't have to send cards. They don't have to do anything special because some woman will compromise and accept anybody just so they don't have to be alone. As if the presence of God just won't do. If men and women who profess to be Christians ever fall in love with the LORD, being alone will be last thing on their respective minds.

This college educated lady I just described was so spiritually disconnected that what she unconsciously said she wanted was *a non-Christian man going nowhere in life who happens to live close by.*

Don't laugh because this is what she has basically said she wants by explaining what she didn't want. If you love Jesus Christ you should be fanatical about it. All you men who love God, don't ever compromise your love of Christ for ANYBODY. My philosophy is don't chase them, but let God replace them. There are many Christians who want to believe in Jesus Christ as long as it doesn't interfere with their life.

If you believe in Christ that's exactly what is supposed to happen. Women please understand that men will always the primary target of Satan. He will attack the woman but he knows the man is the key. You will stand a better chance at a fruitful relationship if your man loves God. Remember that when Eve ate of that forbidden fruit, the only person under condemnation was she. However, when she passed it to Adam and he ate the whole world immediately fell under condemnation.

The devil knows if he can destroy the man he can destroy the family. This doesn't matter if the man is single or not. If he is single the devil will have him jumping from bedroom to bedroom not thinking about settling down with one woman for one minute of his life. Now if you don't think that kind of behavior has a domino effect on all of us just take a look around.

Therefore, it is extremely important that women elevate the standards it takes for a man to gain access to any of her assets. This starts with making sure he has a perfect heart for God. He is not perfect but he is the kind of man who will love you through Christ. He won't run out on you in your time of need. He'll be faithful through thick and thin.

He will be there to comfort you during the rough times. These men will be willing to die for you as Jesus died for us. So we must change our minds. We must change our hearts. Then we can change our conduct. When both men and women make these changes, the kind of men that women are expecting will be the kind women that men will be approaching.

The woman I met will find the kind of man she is looking for because they are out there waiting in the bushes. They are slithering around today just as they were in the garden. As attractive as she was physically she became that unattractive in my eyes spiritually. I began to question what I ever saw in the woman in the first place.

Oh yea, I saw the glitter and the green grass.

TWO
The Odd Couple

*...whosoever shall put away his wife,
saving for the cause of sexual immorality,
causeth her to commit adultery: And
whosoever shall marry her that is
divorced commiteth adultery.* (Matthew 5:32)

One of the most interesting stories in The Old Testament occurs in 1 Samuel 25. David who has been anointed king has been on the run from King Saul. David is the first man in a second position. He has found himself in Carmel, south of Hebron, holed up with six hundred trusted warriors.

He and his men have been guarding the possessions of a wealthy sheep master of Maon named Nabal. David sends ten of his men to Nabal requesting food. Nabal refused. He actually was downright disrespectful to the Man of God.

Now the name Nabal means, "foolish", and he lived up to his name or rather lived down to it. However, during his life of foolishness he found time to make one wise decision that would save the lives of many men.

He married a beautiful God-fearing woman named Abigail. Her

name means, "Father of Joy." Abigail was not only beautiful but she was wise. Her husband had made a tragic error in rebuffing the request of David. She being a godly woman was well of aware of the good intentions of David and his merry men. David's Robin Hood actions of guarding Nabal's sheep were not uncommon in this day. It was unwritten that in this situation it was only right that David should be compensated.

STANDING BY YOUR MATE

Sensing the impending danger her husband and his servants were in she made haste to right this terrible wrong. Let's take a peek at what Abigail did.

Then Abigail made haste and took two hundred loaves, and two bottles of wine, and Two bottles of wine, and five sheep ready dressed, and five measures of parched corn, And a hundred clusters of raisins, and two hundred cakes of figs, and laid them on Asses. And she said unto her servants, go on before me; behold, I come after you. But She told not her husband Nabal. (1 Samuel 25:18-19)

This fascinating and wonderful story is a mirror of many relationships in the church today. There are many couples in the church that have found themselves in this very same situation. On many occasions the godly man or woman has found themselves interceding for the ungodly spouse in the face of God. I could not write a book without addressing an issue I know needs to be addressed. This may not apply to singles but many Christians are experiencing this dilemma.

In this particular scenario I am addressing couples that have married while both people were unsaved. During their marriage one party became converted and began a new life clothed in the Righteousness of Christ.

An internal issue arises with the new convert that causes frustration and doubt. There is frustration because the new Christian wants the same new life for their spouse. The doubt surfaces because the thought of leaving if the unsaved doesn't change grows everyday. However, this new life did not call for separation from his or her spouse. It calls for the new proselyte to stand in the gap for their unsaved mate. This is one of the most troubling areas in the church today. Many people seem to want to abandon their spouse once they give their life to Christ. It may seem like the thing to do but it really isn't. The marriage that was entered into is supposed to be an everlasting covenant in the eyes of God. God considers a covenant as holy promise that should never be broken. We would not want to break the covenant we have with our spouse any more than we would want God to break his covenant with us.

Unfortunately, one of the most interesting things that I have noticed since rededicating my life to Jesus is the manner in which some Christians view their marriage once they become saved. Statistics are showing that the divorce rate in this country is at an all time high and these statistics reflect what is happening inside and outside the church. Now as a saved man of God I am not at all surprised by the numbers of the non-Christians, but the numbers regarding the people who are suppose to be setting the example of God is becoming appalling.

I have found there are several reasons why we Christians are failing just as miserable as non-Christians in the ministry called marriage.

On problem I have found is that Christians tend to use God's Word in a liberal fashion. They find scripture that fits their situation and use it as an escape clause. They have accepted Christ as their Savior but have not taken the next step. That step encompasses one to make him LORD. Upon making him Savior and LORD we then begin living our lives according to the entire doctrine of the Bible.

This means allowing God to reveal who you were and who he wants you to become through his Word. For example many new Christians sometimes rush into marriage once they feel that is what the church would have them do. They never allow God to lead their lives through the study and prayer. These individuals are saved but are still making decisions like they're not.

A Christian man may not be marriage material but feels an insatiable urge to tie the not. This can come from guilt, lust, or church pressure. The person has never dealt with the fact he is not ready for a relationship much less a marriage. Now a man that possesses this type of flaw would be making a grave mistake to give his life to Jesus, and upon meeting the first saved, sanctified, holy ghost filled woman, assume that God has put the two together for holy matrimony.

As crazy as this sounds it happens all the time. The man in this instance feels this will free him of having to deal with habitual sexual sin. The woman is happy because she is blessed with her dream mate. They have spent an earth rocking three months together dating then rush into marriage expecting a life filled with marital bliss.

I am not at all saying this could not happen but more often than not it doesn't. This scenario is played out just as I have indicated and unfortunately when all the dusk clears the married couple wakes up one morning and realize they don't even know each other.

The woman more often than not may find that the man was never serious about living a life sold out for God. He soon begins to gravitate to his old natural man ways. His conscience is seared and he begins to forsake everything the Word of God says. The woman is standing there dazed and confused as if she has taken a boxer's uppercut. What do you do?

This is not an abnormal scenario in the house of prayer. These hazardous unions are the kind that cut at the moral fabric of the church. They refuse to accurately reflect what the people of God think marriage is all about.

MARITAL WOES

Many homes have found themselves in this exact predicament suffocating under the constant strain to remain obedient to God and not depart. Decaying internally at the thought of remaining in a dead-end marriage.

I have personally witnessed this most difficult situation and have even been asked to advise what to do and what not to do. When asked what I think the believing partner should do, there is never a doubt in my mind that we should always investigate through God's precious word.

If any brother hath a wife that believeth not, and she be pleased to dwell with him, let Him not put her away (divorce her). And the woman which hath a husband that Believeth not, and if he be pleased to dwell with her, let her not leave him. For the Unbelieving husband is sanctified by the wife, and the unbelieving wife is sanctified by The husband: else were your children unclean; but now are they holy. (1 Corinthians 7:12-14)

When there is ever doubt to what the godly should or should not do, let the Word of God always be your final authority. Please pay special attention to the word let in the scripture. It is important to know that you must purpose it in your heart to go to the bible for the final word.

Many people have made fatal errors by leaning to their own understanding or worse taking the ungodly counsel from friends, family, or co-workers. We must allow God's Word to rule our entire life to achieve results.

As I mentioned earlier there are many directions these relationships can eventually go. I have seen wives leave husbands and husbands leave wives. I have seen couples remain together and the believer continue their spiritual ascent. The unbeliever will eventually turn from a life of serving the devil and give his or her life to Jesus.

Likewise, ye wives, be in subjection to your own husbands; that, if any obey not the Word, they also may without the(a) word be won by the conversation (conduct) of the Wives; While they behold your chaste conversation (conduct) coupled with fear. (1 Peter 3:1-2)

Although, God is addressing the wives these scriptures are quite appropriate for husbands as well. God says when you as a believer conduct yourself in a godly manner your unbelieving spouse will have the greatest witness. This witness is your life.

When the unbeliever witnesses the change that is taking place through knowing the Savior it will provoke him/her to want to investigate. If a husband/wife believer was cankerous, hateful, greedy, impatient, unforgiving, or lazy, and then begins a metamorphosis right in the very presence of the unbeliever this becomes the most telling truth of the wonderful working power of the LORD.

An old wise mother once said, "Every Child Of God Should Be A Witness For Christ, And When Necessary Use Words." What a profound and wise statement. This truly is advice we can all receive regardless of our situation.

Abigail displayed the kind of character and behavior a husband or wife should routinely display when cohabitating with an unbelieving spouse. She displayed loyalty and compassion for the man she had made a lifelong vow with. She obviously knew her husband and was not surprised by his actions. There was no hesitation on her part to what she should do to rectify the situation. It is extremely important one does not become pious or self-righteous when he/she gives their life to the LORD while the spouse remains unsaved.

You made a promise that the only thing you would allow to come between you and your mate would be death and only death. That vow takes on a more profound meaning now that you are a child of God. In the eyes of God the meaning is the same whether you are saved or unsaved. However, the ungodly seem to throw caution to the wind, and if things don't work they just run out. They have no desire to stick it out with a spouse when differences arise.

But the godly are not suppose to treat their marriages in this manner. Regardless of how foolish our spouses may become we are suppose to pray and turn it over to the LORD. The LORD can change the entire complexity of the relationship but man can't. This is why Abigail and Nabal proved to be such a wonderful example of how a godly person should treat their ungodly spouse.

REPAIRING THE BREACH

We see in First Samuel how Abigail loaded up the donkeys and went out to meet David. When she me him she dismounted and fell before him requesting mercy for her deranged husband. This is what a godly spouse is required to do. The behavior she displayed toward David is the behavior the believing spouse should display toward God. We should be praying daily and seeking the power of God to produce a change of heart of the ungodly spouse. The commitment to the marriage should be elevated now that the love of God is shed abroad in the believer's heart. Though you may not be able to change your spouse rest in peace knowing that God has the power to do it.

Prayer is the outlet to God to let him know you are committed to the saving of the soul of your spouse. Once the person gives their life to God the growth in this new and improved marriage will take care of itself. It will not be perfect but it can take the shape of a marriage God could be proud of. The most important aspect of all this is to remember it may take time. Notice what Abigail did and said when she met David.

And when Abigail saw David, she hasted, and lighted off the ass, and fell before David On her face, and bowed herself to the ground. And fell at his feet, and said, Upon ME, My lord, upon ME let this iniquity be: and let thine handmaid, I pray thee, speak in thine Audience, and hear the words of thine handmaid. Let not my lord, I pray thee regard this man of Belial, even Nabal: for as his name is, so is he; Nabal is his name, and folly Is with him: but I thine handmaid saw not the young men of my lord, whom thou didst Send. I pray thee, forgive the trespass of thine handmaid: for the LORD will certainly Make my lord a sure house; because my lord fighteth the battles of the LORD and evil Hath not been found in thee all thy days. (1 Samuel 25:24-25, 28)

This was the perfect example how a spouse should be willing to stand in the gap and intercede for their mate. This should happen regardless of race, color, or creed. If you are a Christian you should always be willing to do as Abigail did. She approaches David and says lay this charge on my account. What a mighty woman of God. We could all glean from this act of bravery.

I know there are and will be many instances when an ungodly spouse will utter vain words about your newfound faith and even blaspheme the very name of God, but you must not take things into your own hands or moth. Take it to God immediately and petition God to lay the charge on *your* account. I know God must and will judge every man for his own actions, but I am talking about you going to God and pleading for the one thing God has an abundance of and that is MERCY.

Moses did this very thing on countless occasions for the children of Israel. The Israelites had been delivered from Egypt and Pharaoh. However, they began a never-ending habit of complaining to and about God. Rather than allow God to destroy the people Moses stood in the gap for the people. This act of Moses came after God offered to make him a great nation.

Moses was not seeking personal glory because he knew the importance of intercession. Regardless of our marital status we must always remember we are called to intercede for people. Whether they are Christians or not we should never forget this lifelong obligation. God expects this of us since he delivered us out of darkness into his marvelous light.

Abigail understood this obligation completely. She coupled this obligation with the vows she took and was willing to give up her life for her foolish husband. When Nabal should have been willing to give up his life, his wife was out front flipping the script. There is so much in that but I will address it later. She was willing to do this knowing he was a wrong and foolish. She also knew this presented her with a couple of options.

Had she not interceded David and his men would have killed Nabal and all the men in his household. This could have freed her from this marriage instantly. The odd couple would have dissolved and Abigail would have been a free and wealthy woman. But Abigail never thought of this for one moment. Once she realized what had happened she simply sprung into action. Abigail knew it would do no good to talk to Nabal so she took matters in her own hands.

This is what must be done anytime an unbelieving spouse is doing something you know is opposite to what God would have them do. Sometimes it must be done not just for the spouse's sake, but must be for the sake of the entire family. Remember Paul says in 1 Corinthians

7:14, "The unbelieving husband or wife is sanctified by the believer."

Now he is not saying the person is automatically born again into the family of God. What he is saying is from a positional sense the unbeliever is in line to share of the same benefits and blessings of the believer. This position comes from being in a home with a godly person and thus conversion is much more likely.

I know many couples in the church that decided to throw in the towel on an unbelieving spouse and delayed the saving of the unbeliever. This is definitely not the avenue God would have wanted and it ends up sending a terrible message to the church and to the world. The church is supposed to be the standard bearers in which God can use to direct the world. God wants to speak to the world about every subject of life through the church family.

The problem with speaking to the world when we refuse to yield to God's word and begin doing things our way. Notice I said I know many instances in which the believing spouse left the unbeliever. If I were a betting man I would have thought I knew more cases in which the unbeliever left but I cannot honestly say I do. I feel this stems from not knowing and completely understanding God's word. In addition, it comes from not willing to be patient and allow God to work his wonderful miracle working powers.

In addition, it stems from using God's grace as a means to escape a relationship one may have felt was heading south anyway. Notice what the Word of God says in these few scriptures of Psalm 78.

God says in verse one, "Give ear, O my people, to my law: incline your ears to the words of my mouth." God says if you are willing to hear then I am willing to speak. He goes on to say in verses six through eight "That the generation to come might know them, even the children which should be born; who should arise and declare them to their children. That they might set their hope in God, and not forget the works of God, but keep his commandments: And might not be as their fathers, a stubborn and rebellious generation; a generation that set not their heart aright, and whose spirit was not steadfast with God."

What God is simply telling us is this. As life goes on people will get old and begin to die. But before they die off they should diligently seek to teach the next generation all the commandments of God. Why? So as the people of God die off the work of God doesn't.

PURPOSE OF GOD

This is why marriage and family are so vital to God's earthly purpose. You now understand why people who fail to incline their ear to the Word of God usually cause the body of Christ the most shame. If you want to stem the tide of divorce amongst the people of God then all married couples need to hearken to the immutable Word of our Living God.

Regardless of the myriad of reasons that divorce is occurring the church must understand the significance of obeying all of God's word all the time. Partial obedience is total disobedience. It was partial obedience that forced God to snatch kingship from Saul and anoint David the new king. God sees disobedience as a serious offense and must judge it accordingly. God considers marriage on earth as the physical representation of the spiritual union between Jesus Christ and His church. This is why obedience is vital. Can you imagine if Jesus decided to divorce us once we were married to him? Our feeble minds do not begin to allow us to think in these terms. It would the worst day in the history of the world. But because of the covenant God made this will never happen. Thus, we see how important a covenant really is. It is what has us eternally fused together with God.

Not just after we die but we rest now knowing that because of the covenant we will forever be with the LORD. Therefore, the marriage union on earth is should to mirror the union of his only begotten Son to the body of believers. Brethren, God doesn't take kindly to being embarrassed and we shouldn't be nonchalant in our attitude about embarrassing him.

The Old Testament on many occasions referred to the children of Israel as a bride. He refers to the church in the New Testament with the same word. This becomes important as we mature in understanding our marriage vows. It helps us to understand something I want everyone to know. God takes marriage seriously.

Now notice what David said to Abigail after she pleaded for mercy for her husband Nabal. These are such powerful scriptures that attest to what can be accomplished when we submit to the lordship of Christ and obey his word with all our heart.

And David said to Abigail, Blessed be the LORD God of Israel, which sent thee this Day to meet me: And Blessed be thy advice, and Blessed be thou, which hast kept me This day from coming to shed blood, and from avenging myself with mine own hand. For in very deed, as the LORD God of Israel liveth, which hath kept me back from Hurting thee, except thou hadst hasted and come to meet me, surely there had not been Left unto Nabal by the morning light any that pisseth against the wall. (1 Samuel 25:32-34)

David said if you had not come out and interceded for your husband I would have killed every male in his household. Her godly actions not only saved Nabal, but her actions spared the innocent lives of every male in his camp. These other men had no say in whether the goods would be dispersed to David and his men. Nevertheless, they were put in harm's way because of Nabal's hateful decision.

It's because of these type of hateful decision many innocent people lose their money, houses, cars, and even their lives. Everyday wicked people make selfish decisions and when no one intercedes tragedy strikes.

I honestly believe that if God's people would spend more time reading his word and developing a deeper relationship with him they would be in a more submissive position. This position would put them in line to know when the time is right to step in as Abigail did. You are going to read many times where I refer to the importance of studying the Bible so get used to it!

I know someone is asking what if the unbelieving spouse just never softens his or her heart toward God? What if they refuse to turn to God and begin making the believers life a living hell?

1 Peter 2:9 says, "The Lord knoweth how to deliver the godly out of temptations, and to reserve the unjust unto the day of judgment to be

punished." Nabal would very soon after Abigail's encounter with David succumb to death after ten days of illness. This opened the door for David, the future King of Israel to take the beautiful and godly Abigail as his wife.

Now don't go running to your pastor, family, and friends with a prophecy referring to your spouse dying if you are in the situation. If you have found yourself fused together with an ungodly person remain steadfast in your relationship to God. Faithfulness to God opens up doors you could never open up yourself. Always view your marriage as being faithful to God first and the spouse second. God will find a way to make things right just as he did for Abigail. I am not saying that this is the way things normally happen but life has a way of working out for the godly.

Now let me touch on something that I find to be appalling especially when it's said to me. It is when one Christian tells another that their marriage is an impending event. I'm sure you all have heard those ear tingling words come from the mouth of a Christian. You know the "God told me you're my future spouse" phrase so many Christians easily use. This has become the most over-stated line in the history of the church. It is simply amazing how people can always get a word of prophecy in regards to their future spouse, especially when that future spouse belongs to someone else.

They seem to forget the person is married already. The also forget that God never gives any prophecy that contradicts his written Word. Therefore, these types of prophetic utterances should be cast in the sea of lies. Why? God hates divorce. I'll say it again. God hates divorce. If God hates divorce how could someone else's spouse be yours? Let me direct your attention to a scripture you may want to think about the next time you get in a prophetic mood.

...the prophet, which shall presume to speak a word in my name, which I have not commanded him to speak, or that shall speak in the name of other gods, even that prophet shall die. (Deuteronomy 18:20)

UNNATURAL BEHAVIOR

I have seen more cases than I care to see of a married person getting a divorce. Then within weeks or months the person is marrying someone else. What's even more disturbing is the new spouse is usually right in the same church house. I don't think it takes a genius to put this puzzle together. And in many instances church leadership is fully aware of what is going on and never blink an eye.

It is behavior such as this that corrodes the moral fiber of the church and make a mockery of God. Singles must realize that if God can take care of your biggest problem, Salvation, he can definitely connect you with a mate. We must resist taking things in our own hands because there are consequences and repercussions for every action. It is a wonder why the world laughs at us. We are the closest that some people will ever come to seeing Jesus Christ. Therefore, our behavior inside and outside the church should reflect this.

Yes, it is true David ended up with Abigail, but it was through no scheming on the part of the Man of God. God is able and if you truly believe this then hold fast to your profession and exercise patience. There unfortunately will be people who for whatever reason end their marriages.

And though I am not advocating or supporting divorce it happens in our society. God knew that if people would rebel against HIM then rebelling against each other would be no problem at all.

Nevertheless, if you have gone through a divorce do not allow anyone to tell you that you cannot be forgiven. Sin is sin in the eyes of God. You do not have to live your life imprisoned by this one particular mistake in your life. The Bible says in 1 John 1:9, "If we confess our sins, he is faithful and just to forgive us our sins, and cleanse us from all unrighteousness." The only stipulation is we approach him with a heart of repentance. Never approach God with a prideful attitude. We must always come to God without any hint of arrogance while displaying a contrite heart. When we remove all of these internal negatives then we allow him to replace it with genuine love and wisdom. This exchange allows us the strength to move forward with our life.

It will also open up the possibility of marrying again. If we do not allow God to purge the old thoughts and habits we obtained from the first marriage, we will only carry those same hurts and scars to the next. It then becomes a cycle that never ends. And if we have children they pick up on these behaviors and carry them forever.

Boys will grow up seeing there mother with different men and assume that is how women should be treated. They will spend their entire lives jumping from one woman to another never feeling satisfied. The moment something goes wrong or doesn't go according to their plan they will seek to immediately replace rather than restore. This becomes a cycle that is pass from one generation to another. Girls see this behavior in the home and think it okay to live a life having multiple partners. They develop the mind-set that if momma can do it why can't I? This behavior can sometimes find the girl having several children from several men. If these partners prove to be more irresponsible than the woman, they will surely leave the children stranded.

There will be no financial, moral, or emotional support for the children or the mother.

Do you see how this cycle spins its nasty little web? This is why we must understand what we do has an effect on countless people. If you raise a boy or girl who fit this scenario, and release them into society what do you think you have done? There will always be results stemming from everything we believe. Our belief system whether you believe it or not begins right at conception. This is why women have prenatal care.

The prefix pre means before the birth of the child. Any and all steps are taken to ensure a healthy child is birthed into the world. Doctors want to do everything they can to prevent any problems. If we take these measures while the baby is not even visible then doesn't it make much more sense to elevate our care during postnatal care?

During the Sermon on the Mount Jesus told us to let our light so shine before men that they may see our good works and upon seeing those good works give glory to Almighty God.

Every facet of our lives should bring glory to the Father. There will be some things that are out of our control. I am keenly aware of that, but any and every thing we have control of should reflect God's glory in our lives. Therefore, we should seek God in all things and he will provide answers. Relationships are very difficult and I have learned from experience how difficult they can be. My pastor once talked about finding mentors and stated that mentoring is men touring each other's lives. That has stuck with me for a long time.

What I have been able to glean from that is we need to find people whom we can learn from and lean on. I truly believe as Christians we should be involved in a personal three-fold relationship at all times. We should be helping younger people by being mentors for them. We should have a peer group in which we can mentor one another. And we should have someone who is mentoring us. I feel it would be better if we knew the people instead of finding so-called celebrities. The problem with looking to celebrities is if you don't have an actual relationship with them you may find yourself disappointed with them one day.

They are people just like you are and there issues may be worse than your issues. I am referring to people whom you actually are able to have personal contact with. There are quite a few people whom the LORD has sent me for this sole purpose. This sometimes entails nothing more than providing a shoulder to lean and sometimes cry on. This usually helps me more than it helps them.

I have been blessed to have a brother and uncle who have wonderful marriages. Having the opportunity to witness the marital success they enjoy gives me hope. I am usually blessed by how they both handle adversity more than anything else. I am finding out that anyone can navigate the ship when the sea is calm. It's being able to navigate the ship during the storm that keeps the marriage together.

In addition, I have older and wiser people who God has placed in my life to steer me clear of the pitfalls that seem to always lie in wait. I know these tough times are coming and having godly wisdom I can refer to turn is always a plus for me. There wisdom has helped me avoid potential problems I would have otherwise been forced to face. But more importantly when I found myself in the midst of a storm, they helped me get out quicker than I would have on my own. This has proven to be invaluable support as I navigate through the storms of life.

These are a few things we can do to better ourselves and help our fellow man. Let me say this to all who have decided to support this work and read this book. Life is tough. There will be no one standing around with a box of tissue feeling sorry for us. This is why we need the LORD.

This is also why we must seek his counsel and people who live by his counsel. There will be questions and concerns everyday of our entire life. I am truly honored he gave me the opportunity to pen this work. I have found it has spoken to me in more ways than one. I didn't have the benefit of being raised by a mother and father. But I never dwelt on that for one moment.

Many people tend to dwell on what they are missing rather than what they have. That is one reason I feel God had me pen this particular chapter. It does you absolutely no good at all to worry about what you don't have. You had a husband and now you don't. You had a wife and now you don't. Regardless of the reason, you can move on with your life. If you are a widow or widower get in God's face and request he give you peace. Your restoration begins right there. If you are ever going to move forward and remarry this is where it will begin. There are Christians who are still living on past memories of a departed spouse. This is what is called unnatural sorrow. Look at what God says about this.

To every thing there is a season, and a time to every purpose under the heaven: A time To be born, and a time to die; a time to plant, and a time to pluck up that which is Planted; A time to kill, and a time to heal; a time to break down, and a time to build up; A time to weep, and time to laugh; a time to mourn, and a time to dance. (Ecclesiastes 3:1-4)

We are not supposed to sorrow like those who have no hope. Yes we should grieve for the lost of a spouse but that grieving period is not infinite. When David sinned with Bath-sheba his child was struck with an illness that would eventually take its life. David fasted and mourned all night long. He bewailed which such sorrow his men feared telling him when the child actually died. But what David did upon learning of the death of the child is an example for us all. When he learned the child had died, he immediately arose from the ground, washed and anointed himself, changed his clothes, and got something to eat. Well I be dog gone!

That is totally opposite of what I see today when a loved one is lost. David understood that there was a time for praying. He didn't know if God would spare the child or not but he decided to seek God for mercy anyway. However, once the child had died he realized God had made his decision. And though the child was gone David knew that he would one day see the child again. This is so wonderful I'm getting excited just writing.

When you know in the depths of your spirit you are saved you won't allow depression to overtake you when a loved one dies. You know that one day you will see that person again. There are exceptions of course and I'll sadly explain. The Bible says in 2 Corinthians 7:10, "Godly sorrow worketh repentance to salvation not to be repented (regretted) of: but the sorrow of the world worketh death."

What God says in this scripture is powerful and important stuff. I'll give you another example using David. His son Absalom rebelled against him and decided to revolt and overtake the king's throne. During this hostile takeover Absalom was slain. When David learned of the death of this son he cried and grieved with a loud voice. What was the difference? It is why the gospel must be preached. The difference was not with David but with the spiritual state of the two sons. David knew his newborn son would be in the presence of God after death. However, he knew his ungodly son Absalom would not. When people mourn and grieve past the time of sorrow it can only mean one of two things.

They either know in their heart that the loved one was not saved or they themselves are not saved. There may be disagreements but you reserve the right to disagree. But ask yourself a question. What stand do you take in disagreeing? If you are truly saved and understand we all are going to die one day why would you ever sorrow unnaturally. Why would you ever be paralyzed by death when the Bible tells you what is going to happen. Either you believe God and live your life standing on his promises or you don't.

Christians have absolutely no reason to grieve for long periods of time. The scripture in Corinthians explains this clearly. God says godly sorrow worketh repentance to salvation not to be repented or regretted of. Many times at a funeral a preacher will knowingly try and eulogize an ungodly person into heaven. It may sound nice but if that person did not give his or her life to Christ while living nothing you can say will change his or her destination. What God is saying in the first half of this scripture is rather than knowingly lie, the preacher should use this opportunity to warn people that one day we all are going to be in this horizontal position and the time to decide what your destination should be is now. Don't die and expect some speaker to preach or pray you into heaven because it will be too late.

The end of that scripture gives a view of how ungodly folk handle the death of a loved one. They have no hope for the future so they can only see their life here on earth thus they sorrow for days, months, and even years.

For Christians to hear Jesus is coming back is an expected promise but for the ungodly it is a threat. The only thing that means to them is judgment so they want to enjoy this life the best they can. God says they are past feeling and their hearts are blinded. If you have made up your mind to never marry again then at least get to work witnessing for Christ. Don't allow your life to be cut short by being a fruitless tree. Prove you are wise by becoming a soul winner if you aren't already.

When my father passed away in 1998 I didn't cry one tear during the memorial service. I knew then that I was blessed by the time God had given us together while he was here. We both had an opportunity to spend more time together and if we didn't take advantage of it we had no one to blame but ourselves. There were people at the service I had never met before. During my speech I begged them to not let it take the death of another family member to bring us all together again.

That was all I had to give them. No promises, prophecy, or sermons.

What I do know is that I will do everything in my power to point them to Christ while we are alive. So if you are going to disagree with me you will be disagreeing with God and his eternal Word.

I said all that to give some comfort and relief to those who have lost a spouse. The Bible says in Proverbs 27:6, "Faithful are the wounds of a friend; but the kisses of an enemy are deceitful." When people tell you a lie to sooth your feelings, they are not helping you and they are definitely not your friend. Friends will take risk and tell you the truth even if the truth hurts.

True friends hurt to help and not help to hurt. We should never with intended malice tell anybody anything. When it comes to life changing advice I want the truth and not flattery. See Gossip is what someone says to you behind your back they wouldn't say to your face, but flattery is what someone will say to your face they wouldn't say behind your back. Just tell me the truth and let me deal with it. This is why I get in trouble. Since this what I expect I tend to give it the same way. I am learning like we all must learn when and how to pick our spots.

I truly hope this will free the mind of someone who has been holding on to the past. Don't put yourself in the position where years go by and you end up looking back in regret. You can move on and regain the experience that comes with the love and passion of godly marriage. God can use your life as a testimony for all those people who don't think they have anything to offer HIM. There is simply nothing God can't do in your life. The billion-dollar question is do you want it?

THREE

IF IT'S NOT GOD'S WILL, IT'S GOD'S WON'T.

Thou Shalt Not Take Thee A Wife,
Neither Shalt Thou Have Sons Or Daughters
IN THIS PLACE. (Jeremiah 16:2)

I was perusing through a popular secular magazine and came across an article that was introducing two new terms the twenty-first century culture are beginning to embrace.

The two new terms caught my attention because they mirror what God's word says about the subject they represented. The terms suggested a sense of respect and self-control that is required as a man or woman grows in their relationship with God.

The terms were similar in that they were derived from the same word. They were different because each one represented both respective genders. So I assume you would like to know what the name of the terms were?

The terms were called, "Manticipation" and "Womanticipation." Now I have to assume you would like for me to explain what they mean?

These terms were referring to the act of a man or woman

suppressing their desire to have sexual relations with their unmarried partner to the breaking point of their emotions. This was done in order to increase the fulfillment and pleasure once they decide to suppress no more.

You say how does this relate to the Word of God? Well God says sexual relations should be for two married individuals. Therefore, if two people are dating this is exactly what they should be doing. They should be using the controlling work of the Holy Spirit to suppress any sexual desires they may have until they decide to suppress no more.

When should this time be? This time should occur after both the man and woman say "I DO." I found the article to very interesting because it ceases to amaze me what unsaved people tend to do in order to bring happiness and joy into their lives. The article never addressed marriage as an option during the dating process and never addressed the repercussions of what would happen after suppressing had ceased. It never discussed the sanctity of the act instituted by God himself. And it never came close to discussing the positive aspects that could occur from abstaining from the act of sex period.

I found this to be quite depressing. This article enhanced my desire to continue writing this book because the people of God really need to understand that if it's not God's will it's God's won't.

God told Jeremiah the prophet in the sixteenth chapter of the book of Jeremiah, "Not to take thee a wife, neither shalt thou have sons or daughters IN THIS PLACE." Now notice that I intentionally capped three of God's words to the prophet. I think these words will help me to help you by explaining some important things we should know. If I would stop at that one scripture and begin a narrative explaining these things I would truly be doing a disservice to the subject. Therefore, lets go further to lay the foundation to a spiritual truth that will play an important role in my summation.

Thou shalt not take thee a wife, neither shalt thou have sons or daughters in this place. For thus saith the LORD concerning the sons and daughters that are born in this place, And concerning their mothers that bare them, and concerning their fathers that begat Them in this land; They shall die of grievous deaths; they shall not be lamented; neither Shall they be buried; but they shall be dung upon the face of the earth: and they shall be Consumed by the sword, and by famine; and their carcases shall be meat for the fowls Of heaven, and for the beasts of the earth. (Jeremiah 16:2-4)

That's pretty strong stuff from God to the prophet but there are some important lessons in which we can glean and learn. The first and most important spiritual truth is that God sees our entire life while we see a snapshot. I titled this chapter the way I did because as singles it is extremely important that we must always be discerning spiritually to know when God calls us not to do things.

God could have just told Jeremiah not to marry and ended the conversation. Believe me God has been know to give commands without giving reasons. He may come back and eventually give you a soothing reason as to why he laid down a specific commandment, be he'll do it on his own time.

For example, in the Book of Corinthians the apostle Paul had to ask the LORD three times to remove the thorn from his flesh. It took three times before God even cleared his throat to answer Paul and when he did answer, it wasn't what Paul wanted to hear. Paul wanted the thorn removed and God offered an alternative named GRACE.

So we have to understand that God knows us better than we could ever know ourselves. He has a destiny and purpose for each of our lives and he must convey to us the importance of choosing whom will be part of that destiny and plan. Left up to us we would be like a yellow cab picking up every thumb waving pedestrian and carrying all of them along for a ride God did not intend for them to take.

Discernment is one of the most important elements of our spiritual growth. We must learn to exercise and perfect it if we intend to avoid unnecessary pitfalls. I know from my own experience that there have been times prior and even after my one on one encounter with the LORD, that I made choices not based on what I thought God wanted but what I thought would work best for my particular situation. And in all those instances I made choices that turned out to be wrong. It wasn't that I committing blatant sin against God in these instances. Nevertheless, I still found myself derailed off the rode in which God had me on.

The prophet Jeremiah was given a commandment from God and subsequent reasoning into why the commandment was given. Jeremiah could not see that having a wife and family would not be only a burden but would also cause him to lament and bemoan them had they been IN THIS PLACE.

Remember I capped those three words for a reason. Now if you read the entire text baring the prophet Jeremiah's name you know he never did marry but that is not what I am saying God requires for all or any of us. However, there can and will be reasons you will find yourself single that have nothing to do with you or your personhood.

I sincerely believe Christians should not be dating seriously if marriage is not where they are headed. I also believe God feels the same way. When we date with no godly end in sight we open ourselves up to temptations that can only be fulfilled by the flesh. However, when a man and woman date with a common goal of one day glorifying God by partaking in the wonderful institution of marriage, we have a foundation built by God date by. And why does God want Christian men and women married? To produce godly children who will in turn produce godly children.

IN THIS PLACE were the key words in verse two of the chapter in Jeremiah's book. God knew what the prophet didn't know just as he knows what we don't. He is keenly aware of what we need and what we don't need. He is acutely aware of when we need it and when we don't. Finally, he is intelligently aware of where we need what we need and where we don't need it. In other words, God knows who, when, where, and how in regards to our lives. He wants us to realize this truth and trust in him always.

Had the place been different God may have permitted Jeremiah to marry, but for that particular time and place taking on a family would not have any benefit to what God had called Jeremiah to do.

This is the key so don't run by that too fast. Note I said it would not benefit what God had called Jeremiah to do. It was obviously something Jeremiah had on his mind and perhaps in his heart. God had called him to be a prophet at the tender age of seventeen and being called out to a work of this magnitude called for some lonely days and nights.

God understood how Jeremiah felt. Remember we don't have a high priest who cannot be touched with the feelings of our infirmities. God knew Jeremiah was longing for companionship that only another human could give him. He had God but that was not what Jeremiah desired. I believe this because God never brings up anything that he doesn't feel the need to bring up.

HEART DESIRES

I don't read in the previous chapter anything about Jeremiah asking God for a wife so I know God who is a discerner of the hearts of men decided to give Jeremiah an answer to a question the prophet had not formed with his mouth.

Believe me when I tell you I can attest to this in my own life. The bible says in the book of Proverbs 19:21, "There are many devices (plans) in a man's heart; Nevertheless the counsel of the LORD, THAT shall stand." As you see God never has to hear you open your mouth to know what you desire in your heart.

But don't despair this is not a mechanism God uses to shoot down every desire that you have in your heart because he also says in Psalm 37:4-5, "Delight thyself also in the LORD; and he shall give thee the desires of thine heart. Commit thy way unto the LORD; trust also in him; and he shall bring it to pass."

Now God won't necessarily give you what you want but he will give you what to want. When you allow God to not only be Savior but the LORD of your life you will begin to discern what he feels you should have and should not have. When you understand what he has predestined for you to do in the earth realm you will begin to understand what is needed and not needed for you to move forward in the admonishment of the LORD.

Many single Christians today are devising many plans that do not line up with what God wants for their lives. I beseech you to start growing in the area of discernment so you can take your mind off of self and put it on God.

When you begin to exercise this spiritual gift you will find yourself delighting in the LORD and the desires of your heart will line up with the desires God has for you.

God says in Matthew 6:33, "To seek First the Kingdom of God, and his Righteousness; and all these things shall be added unto you."

Included in the THESE THINGS is a mate. God knows what you need so there is no need to worry about these things because he has theses things taken care of.

The end of verse five of Psalm 37 says we must trust also in him. We MUST learn to Trust God in every aspect of our lives. I cannot begin to count the times I just knew I met the ONE. You know the woman or man you just knew was your future husband or wife. I had the plans all ready made and then all hell broke loose. I through myself into the relationship with all I had and God intervened.

Let me tell you something God intervenes in human affairs. I thank him immensely for that. And when I look back at the relationships that never panned out I have to give him all the praise because he knew that I did not need that particular woman. God knew based on my personality that the people I chose were not compatible for me. *Praise the LORD.*

I can say this in hindsight but during the period of romance I was blinded by the possibilities of having a wife and family. But I now am growing spiritually and understanding that if I remain focused on God's plans everything will fall into place.

Jeremiah was known as the weeping prophet and he undoubtedly wept over the news God gave him regarding his family expectations. He knew he would be facing a life lonely on earth but fulfilled in the Love of God. You have to ask yourself can you live your life focused totally on God and what he has planned for your life.

I distinctly remember meeting a very attractive young lady and thinking she had the potential to be my wife. I laid down the red carpet by sending flowers to her job and buying cards and candy. Soon after she decided what I wanted was not what she wanted. To say the least I was floored. I now know that because of the plan and purpose God had for my life it was actually God saying NO and not she. And the longer I live and relate to women I am starting to realize that although I may not know who the right woman is, I know who she ain't. I know that's not correct English but that is the best way I know to say it.

You see men have the propensity to choose women based on their physical pulchritude. But while men look on the outside, God looks on the inside. God knows the person who is most compatible for each and everyone of us. I have learned to not kick against the pricks when it comes to choosing a mate. I also feel it necessary to note that many people miss God because they try and discern God through the senses rather than through the Spirit. After the fall of man God cursed Adam and Eve for their disobedience.

However, before he rebuked them he looked right at the serpent and made a promise that would change the course of the world. In Genesis 3:15 God says, "I will put enmity between the woman and thee and between thy seed and her seed: it shall bruise thy head, and thou shalt bruise his heel."

SEE IT IN THE SPIRIT

Now for hundreds and thousands of years this promise was passed from generation to generation. Every woman born would here about the promise Jehovah God made and marvel at the opportunity to become the mother of the future Savior of the world. Everyone knew God's only begotten Son would be coming soon.

Great prophets like Isaiah, Jeremiah, Daniel, and Ezekiel spoke of his coming. So what happens when he finally arrives on the scene? Is there a ticker-tape parade waiting? No. Are there massive celebrations in the Jerusalem synagogues? No. So what awaits our blessed hope? Herod wants to kill him immediately after being born. He grows up in obscurity as the son of a carpenter. His brothers refuse to embrace him as family. And when he finally becomes a man, and after almost four years of teaching, healing, and comforting, what do the very people who anxiously awaited his arrival for so many years do? Reject HIM!

I said all of that to say this about singles in the church. We can expect God to bless us with someone and think we know exactly what we want. But then it shows up not looking like what we think it should look like and what do we do. Instead of embracing the gift we pull out our weapons of defense and commence to beat it. We pull out our carnal weapons and verbally abuse it. We put on our pious and self-righteous face and turn our back on it. Understand the only way you can know what is God's will or won't is to be so spiritually grounded you don't know where God begins and you end.

My beloved, this is going to take work and time. This is why patience is going to have to be a virtue when walking with God. You may have to spend some days, months, or even years alone. But being alone doesn't mean you have to be lonely. As you draw closer to God you will find you were never nor will you ever be lonely again.

There may be times when I may be feeling lonely and depressed but I know that is the time to focus on kingdom business. It is vitally important to not make hasty decisions regarding companions. Never make these decisions while in a lonely or depressed state because if you choose someone during this time you may find yourself regretting that decision in the future. Apart from accepting Jesus Christ as your Savior and LORD, the most important decision you may have to make will be choosing a husband or wife.

Therefore, you must become spiritually mature so that you can immediately know who to accept and who to reject. Always remember God's words, "Thou wilt keep him in perfect peace, whose mind is stayed on thee: because he trusteth in thee." (Isaiah 26:3)

Having therefore these promises we must change our "stinkin' thinkin'." We must recognize what is of God and what is not of God by changing our minds. When we are "born again" we immediately develop a passion to want to tell someone. We search for a roof to yell from and proclaim the change God has made in our lives. Who do you think gives you this new vigor to proclaim and preach about God. That's right the Holy Spirit. Jesus said he would not leave us comfortless or as orphans. When he spoke to the disciples during their last meeting he promised a helper would come alongside to help us.

This same Holy Spirit draws us to Christ and then indwells us after accepting Christ. That right there would be enough to shout about but it doesn't end there.

The Holy Spirit guides and directs the life of the Christian when we submit to his power. The key therein lies with us deciding whose will is going to win. We have been given the same option to freely choose in this life today. God does not take that away from us. He wants us to submit out of love not out of fear or duress. This is why Jesus told us, "If ye love me, keep my commandments." When you keep the commandments of God you don't display a sign of legalism or fear but of love.

I cannot begin to tell you how many times I have unintentionally and intentionally destroyed blessings God had for me. I won't get into specifics but God has had some wonderful opportunities not counting relationships just waiting for me. But because of foolishness on my part I found a way to abort what he conceived. This I remind you has happened since being saved and not only before. This is why I thank God for his Grace and his Mercy. You will experience many instances when you will think you know what is best for you and will talk yourself into believing God said it. God will be nowhere in the conversation and you will make the decision. It will fall apart and rather than admit you made the wrong decision, you will utter what all self-righteous Christians normally say and that is, "I missed God." In actuality you never sought him.

Understand that there are three voices you will hear now that you have been redeemed by the blood of Jesus. One voice you will hear will be God's voice. How he speaks to you is entirely different than how he speaks to any other living person. But his voice only speaks according to his Word. God never has and never will say anything that is opposite of his Word. Therefore, if you have to make any decision you can best believe that if God has given you an answer it will line up with scripture.

The second voice you hear will be the devil. He speaks only lies and will always whisper things in your ear that contradict every scripture in the Word of God. If he happens to quote scripture word for word he will be quoting it for the purpose of lying. He is not to be trusted at any cost. We are to give him no place and flee from any invitations he presents us with. The devil will never invite you to any place, person, or thing that will edify your life. Be aware that this voice may have the body of someone you know. He will use anyone who does not mind being used. Remember that if it's contrary to God's Word it has to be the devil. He has sought to destroy everything God loved from the very beginning and he will not stop until God destroys him on that last judgment day.

The third and final voice you will hear is your own voice. The Bible says, "There is a way that seems right unto a man, but the end thereof is death." Man has a way of coming up with some wicked schemes on his own. He will sit in his laboratory and devise plans and programs that he will put off on God and present them for consumption. When no one bites on the frivolous ideas of a self promoting schemer he or she will say they missed God. Look God is not in the business of blessing man's ideas. God blesses his Word and that is it.

There are people who don't spend one moment of one day thinking about God, yet they are filthy rich. Therefore, never look at the possessions of anybody in the House of God to gauge their spirituality. That is not and never will be the indicator. If you must see physical evidence then pay close attention to their life. If you must go deeper than that, then pay close attention how they spend their time. If you must perhaps go even deeper than that, then pay attention to what they spend their money on. If you must take it even one step further, then pay close attention how they treat God's people!

These are spiritual indicators that never fail. I know professing Christians who never seek God and treat God's people indifferent. And God's people are not just Christians because the Bible says the earth and they that dwell within belong to God. That means Christians should be treating all people the same. God is not a respecter of persons and neither should we be. I know there will be times when people will treat you cold but you don't have to allow them to bring you down to their level. People who do this don't have the secret weapon you have. They don't have the power of the Holy Spirit. And if Christians treat you that way then just all God to handle it.

ORDERED STEPS

While I'm on the subject about the treatment of people it is noteworthy to know that the closer you get to God the further you will get from people. Also, your talk will become ridiculous to the ears of the natural or carnal man. The natural man is a man or woman who is not "born again" and the carnal man is a man or woman saved but allowing them to be led by their flesh. As you become more spiritual you will find yourself gravitating away.

This is not to say you will eventually go off to your own island but you will notice God separating you in order to take you higher. There will be some who will remain close but many will not. The higher Jesus went the smaller his circle became. He only took Peter, James, and John when he went up to the mount and spoke with Moses and Elijah.

When he prayed in the garden of Gethsemane he once again took the same three men. Some will come but many will not. Therefore, understanding that it is God's plan will allow you to have peace. It is not easy to lose the friendship of people you have known for years but that is one of the prices that must be paid to be a disciple for Jesus.

Never more than now have I been able to understand this spiritual truth. I once could rattle off the names of numerous men and women whom I counted as dear friends but I just don't know anymore. My feelings for them have not changed but have actually grown. I pray all the time for my friends, family and even foes. I pray that God would do a miracle working change in their life as he has done in mine. I try to keep communication going as best I can but for some reason there seems to be a breakdown. I wondered many times why did they change on me? Why would they just stop calling? Why would they quit trying to visit? Why have these people just forgot about what we had? But you know what I found out? Although it has taken some time, I realized they didn't stop doing those things but I did.

I had become so preoccupied in trying to learn every scripture, attend every service, and study every tape that I completely forgot to live out what I already knew. I immediately changed that and began reaching out to all of those people who I had ignorantly forgot. Some have reciprocated and some have not, but I have done what God put in my heart and my hands are clean. What I now do is pray and leave it in the hands of the Father. Hallelujah.

Many Christians are guilty of this same thing. They are like hogs sitting at a table with their knife and fork. They are snorting and commanding to be fed. Feed me some more and feed me now. I need more word, more scripture, more tapes, more books, and more religion. Yet, they never do anything with what they already know. They never walk out what God has already blessed them with. They run from church to church and from city to city and from preacher to preacher, and for what. They have not walked out what their own pastor told them the previous Sunday and they have already made plans for the next big conference.

And we wonder why we don't know what God's will and won't is. I know Christians who will buy a plane ticket to a city, book a hotel for a week, rent a car, and pay for a sitter just to go to the next big conference. They will put it on a credit card knowing they can't afford it and say God told me to go. These very same Christians are the very folk who will not tithe nor support their own local pastor or church. God has blessed them with a pastor and a church in which they can attend and serve. They say God told me to go here and God told me to go there. Yet, God has never told them to serve in a ministry, pay tithes, reduce their debt, read the Bible, attend Bible class, or bless the pastor by doing something nice for him or his wife.

God has said everything but these things. Remember I told you God does not and cannot speak against what he has already said in the Bible. That would make God out to be a liar. Now I know there are times God will speak to one's heart to attend a conference in or out of town. But if you have not been faithful in being a faithful servant in your own house. Come on. I shutter to think about this because it happens so frequently and people wonder why they never find themselves in God's will. How would you feel if your child went to the neighbor's house and cut the grass, washed the car, and trimmed the hedges and came right back to your house and sat down and did nothing? Came right back and ate your food, slept in your bed, wore your clothes, and not one time offered to do any chores at his own house.

That is exactly how God feels. That is how the pastor feels. And that is how the people who serve every LORD day feel. Paul said he wanted to know Jesus in the power of his resurrection and the fellowship of his suffering. Paul wanted to experience the wonderful times that came from serving the LORD. He wanted to bask in the wonderful glory of knowing he had preached with all his heart and soul. He wanted to know he had left no stone unturned in his pursuit to spread the gospel.

But Paul also wanted to know what it felt like to be hated for doing those exact things. He reveled in the opportunity to be despised like his savior Jesus Christ. He could not think of any better badge of honor than to have suffered for the sake of Christ. I believe this is why many refuse to allow themselves to be submitted to God's will or God's won't.

Many want to reign with Christ, but God can keep the suffering. Many expect Abraham blessings but display Thomas like faith. Many grope for the face of God then repent and seek his hand instead. These are recipes for a defeated Christian life here on earth. There must be sacrifice or there will be no blessing. The only place success comes before work is in the dictionary.

The Bible says God loves order and commands all things be done decently and in order. When I began paying tithes it put my entire financial life into order. Many Christians say they cannot afford to tithe but I say you cannot afford not to. If your finances are so out of order you feel that way then believe me tithing is the recipe for you. It will force you to list your expenses from most to least important. And when God is placed at the top of that list you will begin to see financial order restored to your life. Jeremiah 29:11 says, "For I know the thoughts that I think toward you, saith the LORD, thoughts of peace, and not of evil, to give you an expected (a future and a hope) end." In addition, he has an everlasting love for his people.

These are words from God himself and if he says these words we should be willing to hang our hat on those promises. Therefore, we should cast all our cares on him and root ourselves in what he has said. Believe me if we possessed the ability to do the things we need to do we wouldn't need God. When we begin to live and not just exist in the world we will not spend one minute worrying about the cares of this world.

There have been and will be times when we will make decisions that may turn out to be completely wrong. Don't allow this to suck your life away. As children of God we must align our hopes with the hope of Christ Jesus. And when you feel your position does not mirror God's position you better change where we're standing. God says in Jeremiah 31:33, speaking of the new covenant that, "he will put his law in our inward parts (mind), and write it in their hearts; and will be their God, and they shall be my people." You see God's entire plan for us is to become so fused together with him that knowing his will for our lives will become second nature.

God knows that whatever captures the mind and heart of the man captures the man himself. Therefore, if God's entire plan can capture our hearts and mind can you imagine the heights we could soar? See the more information we have the better our decision-making will be. What information do we need? The best that's available for us.

GODLY COUNSEL

Biblical information should be the number one priority for a Christian. Once we have saturated our minds with this information we become better equipped to make godly decisions. However, we must know when to act once we receive information. If we are constantly receiving information and never act then the information becomes obsolete.

God never intends for us to be reactors. God never reacts to anything. He always acts. When Satan caused Adam to fall in the garden he know doubt thought he had God whipped. But if you run over to the last book in the Bible you will see that there already was a Lamb slain before the foundation of the world waiting for the fall. God already had the information therefore he was able to act. He didn't have to wait for anything in the garden to transpire before he made his move. This is how the Christian life should be lived. When calamity or blessing come we should look at it and say "I was expecting that." We are commanded to rejoice in all things so when all things show up it should be no surprise. God is patiently waiting for us to get our priorities in order.

One day Jesus was praying and as he finished one of disciples asked him to "teach them how to pray." What is interesting about this is that they had been on missionary trips prior to this particular discussion. They had been healing sick and casting out devils in the name of Jesus.

See you can be doing good works as a Christian and still not know the will of God for your life. You know the will for your life through prayer. Freeing yourself from ignorance received from the world will come through prayer and knowledge of the Truth or Word of God. Jesus begins to teach them the prayer that begins with, "Our Father." One of the most important parts of that prayer is when Jesus says, "Thy will be done on earth as it is in Heaven." When you know what is going on in heaven it will make earth life run much smoother. We must get it into our heads that what is going on in heaven is taking place with expectancy of us. Jesus told us, "I go to prepare a room for you" in my Father's house. That sounds to me as if we are expected to show up and it should sound the same way to you.

I always have to give scripture to support what I say or write because there is so much garbage being preached today. And though I am writing this book directly from my heart, you should know my heart is centered on God and his Word. There have been many people who have told me God has called me to preach and I firmly believe that.

However, that doesn't necessarily mean it must be done from the pulpit. There are many mediums God can use an individual to preach. Writing happens to be one and I am glad about it. But let's say I didn't seek God's will for my gift to preach and just went on an expedition to become a pastor of a church. I could be dragging myself all around this country trying to open a door God has completely shut. And let me tell you when God shuts a door no man can ever open it. This is why it is futile to lose heart over jobs, careers, people, or things. What God has for you he has for you. You have to find out how do you get it.

I have also found that we sometimes get in the will of God for our lives but make the mistake of taking people who are not suppose to be there. In the Book of Acts the Holy Spirit commanded that Paul and Barnabas, two of the giants in the faith, to join together for missionary work. They obeyed albeit with one slight addendum. They took John Mark to be their minister as well. Though John Mark was a talented young preacher he was not called for this particular trip. His time would undoubtedly come for we know he would eventually write the *Gospel of St. Mark*. But this was not his mission and Paul and Barnabas took him anyway. During this mission John Mark would eventually abandon them and return home.

Upon returning and expressing concern about the people they had ministered to Paul decided it would be good to return to see how the people were doing. See there were no phones, faxes, or express mail to use therefore, face-to-face meetings were the order of the day. Barnabas agreed but wanted to take John Mark again. Paul didn't agree and the Bible says that these two great men developed contention between them so sharp they parted ways. Paul would end up choosing Silas and Barnabas took John Mark.

What was the major difference? The Holy Ghost hadn't spoke to anybody. These were decisions made on their own. The Holy Ghost commanded the formation of the team of Paul and Barnabas and because of the intervention of man this is what wound up happening.

If you read the rest of the Book of Acts you will notice after chapter number fifteen you don't read about Barnabas again. Paul would continue on doing mighty works for God that would be permanently recorded. I have no doubt that Barnabas also would go on to do great things but can you imagine what these two could have accomplished had they remained faithful and steadfast in the will of God? I understand Barnabas' position because he was a compassionate man.

He saw something in John Mark the same way he saw something in Paul when he was converted from Saul. No one trusted Paul during the embryo stages of his conversion. No one except Barnabas. But you must remember that Paul was so sold out for Jesus he would go against his own mother if the LORD commanded it.

There will be times when you will know that God has called you to do something and everything you see will give you indication as to who is suppose to go along. You better make sure you take only the people who God has commanded. The reason is that though God didn't call these people, they will follow you as if God had actually called them himself. This is why men must be very careful about who they choose as a mate. The woman must be willing to get on board and take the plan or vision God has given him and see that plan as if God gave it to her. Now do you see why it is so important to know God's will and God's won't? For a woman to be submissive is for her to be submissive when submission is required.

It does a couple absolutely no good if the woman has joined with a man, then in the middle of the game decides to change the rules. To change the rules changes the game and to change the game changes the plan. If the plan came from God how can it be changed? And if the plan cannot be changed how can the game be changed? And if the game cannot be changed how can the rules be changed?

I truly hope you understood what I just stated. This is why it is critical men find wives who can submit not to them, but to God. If a woman is submitted to the will of God and decides to marry, she is agreeing to be submitted to the man.

This kind of talk makes absolutely no sense in the world. The world would think I have completely gone off my rocker to make statements such as this but I'm just repeating what God says. Therefore, the world doesn't have a problem with me they have a problem with our Creator. But ladies answer me this one question? Who would you rather have as the head of your home? A godly man who consistently lives his life and leads his family according to dictates of God's word or would you rather have one of these ungodly jokers who gets tossed to and fro by every new thing that comes his way.

When tough times come he gets his cues from the horoscope page in the local newspaper. He checks out what the latest tabloid magazine suggests. He calls his twice-divorced buddy on the phone for marital advice. And let's not forget his ace in the whole on family advice, the ex-girlfriend who simply adores you.

These are the type of people and things ungodly people refer to when trouble comes. Which man would you want to sleep beside for the next fifty years? Which would you want to have children with someday? Which would you trust with a joint bank account? Think about it because these are questions you may have to ask yourself about a guy kneeling in front of you holding a ring. He may be fine as all get out. He might have more degrees than a thermometer. He may have the most expensive car on the block. He might have a squeaky clean image according to the standards of the world. But what is his standing in relation to God Almighty. Right standing with the world doesn't equate to right standing with God.

I haven't forgot about you guys don't worry. You will have to decide if that drop dead gorgeous lady has a personality compatible to yours. She might have the shape of a pear but what if the pear is rotten? She may make a decent salary but who receives the most, God or the mall? Some of these may sound funny when reading but these are questions many people never ask or ask too late. The consequences are usually relationships destined for failure.

I have purposed in my heart that I want to make sure I am always seeking the will of God for my life. I want HIM to be number one in everything I do. I was recently led to take a closer look into my finances and make a change. I am going to make sure each month the highest amount of money that leaves my account will be to the furthering of the gospel of Jesus Christ. The most money I spend every month will be money I give back to God. This may come through tithes, freewill offerings, love gifts, benevolence, or simply sending checks to ministries I know are proclaiming the Gospel.

These are the things I know are part of the will of God for my life. I honestly feel God is preparing a wife especially for me. Nevertheless, I refuse to just sit around idle until she comes. I don't think so because that is simply not my style. I have other books to write, sermons to preach, people to help, and work to do.

Ecclesiastes 9:10 says, "Whatsoever thy hand findeth to do, do it with thy might; for there is no work, nor device, nor knowledge, nor wisdom, in the grave, whither thou goest." These are the immortal words were written by the wisest king in the history of the world,

Solomon himself. He was wise and rich and yet he said you better get busy doing whatever you are going to do because the grave is waiting. I know people who constantly saying what "I'm about to do" and what "I'm fixing to do." The time for about to and fixing to are over.

I had this book locked up in my heart for two years. It was high time to let this thing out and praise the LORD I have. And guess what: I've only just begun. Some of the best books, songs, ideas, business plans, marriages, hopes, and dreams are in the graveyard. Don't let that happen to you.

I have always said something I think might help some of you. When I am caught in a dilemma I always say I can live with being rejected but I can't live without trying. God doesn't punish godly attempts. There is nothing wrong with trying something you feel is in your heart.

Someone once said "I'd rather fail in a cause which would ultimately succeed than to succeed in a cause which will ultimately fail." Seek God with every fiber of your being and he shall direct your path. It is then when you will fully understand what is God's Will and what is God's Won't for life.

FOUR

JUST WAITING ON THE LORD

...they that wait upon the LORD shall renew their strength; they shall mount up with wings as eagles; they shall run, and not be weary; and they shall walk, and not faint. (Isaiah 40:31)

On many occasions I have asked single men and women why they are still single. And more times than I care to count, I seem to always here the immortal Christian single phrase that is, "I'm Just Waiting On The Lord."

Now don't get me wrong because I completely understand this is what children of God should be doing, but it is usually the conversation that follows that response that puzzles me. Unfortunately, many Christians believe waiting on the LORD is being idle or stagnant. This is a major mistake I would like to address for a few moments.

If something living doesn't move for a long period of time it tends to atrophy and die. This is what many Christians are unconsciously doing sometimes when they are as they say "waiting on the LORD." In the Gospel of Luke Jesus speaks of the parable of the ten pounds and in chapter nineteen and verse thirteen he commands ten servants whom he has given ten pounds each to, "Occupy till I come." Jesus commands these servants in the parable to do business, trade, stay busy, grow, and expand their horizon.

Waiting on the LORD does not mean waiting around wasting time. I truly believe you don't become a husband of wife when you say, "I DO." I believe this transformation occurs before you and your future spouse ever make it to the church or the altar.

As a single man or woman you are presented with freedom in which you will not be able to experience when you enter into the sanctity of marriage. Therefore, this time of freedom you are experiencing is an excellent opportunity to expand and grow. You should ensure you are bringing a 100 percent individual to the marriage. Many people think marriage is 50-50 but that is so wrong.

Marriage is about two complete and whole persons coming together to form a bond that no one will be able to break. The bible says in Colossians chapter two that we are complete in Christ Jesus. This means we have all spiritual blessings in Christ and we need and lacking nothing.

However, these are the spiritual blessings of the LORD. But there are some tangible things we can do to improve educationally, financially, emotionally, and personality wise. Waiting on the LORD as a single man or woman can be one of the most exhilarating times for a Christian. That is if we use the time wisely.

REDEEMING THE TIME

Always remember that the most important asset we have is time. Time is something we can never recapture. We can lose money, friends, cars, homes, jobs, and even family and replace them all. But when we waste the precious commodity of time that God has given, we must remember we will never regain it.

Time is not for sale, lease, or loan. Therefore, it is extremely important and wise to utilize it to the best of our ability. This is why waiting on the LORD is not merely waiting.

I read an article in a popular women's magazine regarding a thirty-four year old virgin. She was a former beauty queen whose parents raised her and her brothers to embrace a lifestyle of abstinence. She never felt like she missed anything by making this decision and what made it easier to do was setting goals and staying busy. She developed educational programs and used this stance to become one of the most sought after women in the country for speaking on this subject.

What I admired about her was that she was not waiting around the house in slippers and a negligee for prince charming. She wasn't expecting him to ride by on his white horse and sweep her off her feet. She decided that if she stayed busy and kept her eye on more pressing matters God would reward her act of chastity.

My point is there are so many things single men and women can be doing while God is preparing that special person for them. One thing we can do is to allow God to prepare us. I know single women who are constantly making the statement that they are ready to get married but their lifestyle tells a completely different story. If a two hundred pound woman decided to lose fifty pounds and her refrigerator was stocked with ice cream, cake, cookies, and soft drinks, I would be very skeptical about her commitment to losing her desired weight.

The same goes for single men and women who always utter the phrase "I'm ready to get married." There are many men who make this statement and still have a nightlife that have them coming home at three and four o'clock in the morning. This alone would raise concern regarding a man of God, but I won't get into that. That's another sermon for another time.

Unfortunately, this and other things are happening in the lives of single men. They say they want to get married but have not kept a solid job for any significant period of time. They change jobs like Texas weather. When someone says or does something they don't like they head for the door. This is inconsistent behavior for someone who claims to be ready for a lifetime commitment.

In addition, there money is always low or non-existent. They're consistently late on one bill and paying half on another. Also, there hygiene lacks attention and their organizational skills are less than desirable. Women in turn utter the same I'm ready for marriage phrase and yet many cannot keep a home together to save their mother's life.

Bathroom items are never fully stocked. The home is never tidy and there is only one person in the house to clean behind. They shop on impulse for wants instead of needs. Their closets are overstuffed with items purchased months ago that were never worn. Cooking is so rare there is never a surplus of groceries, so eating out is always the order of the day. These are men and women who claim they are ready for the responsibility of marriage. For some reason I would expect women to be more prepared than men.

These are just a few of the many areas where improvements can be done to begin lining up the life with the mouth. Singles must understand that God is not going to send one of his kings or queens to them until they are ready to receive that person.

Galatians 6:7 says, "Be not deceived; God is not mocked: for whatsoever a man soweth, that shall he also reap." Remember the aforementioned story about the woman trying to lose fifty pounds? How far do you really think she is going to get in achieving her goal? She has sowed failure by putting the wrong foods in her immediate reach. The same goes for singles Christians who seriously want to be married.

A single man or woman should be so grounded in the idea of being a husband or wife that when people look at their life, they will assume that person is already married. They may be years from making the plunge but their life will resemble someone who already is. I have never been married, but I believe single Christians who desire marriage should begin practicing that lifestyle while they are in fact still single. That's just my opinion but I am living what I preach. I have found that by living this way I make decisions as if I already have a wife and children.

If I can't afford to buy it with cash I don't need it. I don't hang out in the streets at ungodly hours of the night. I choose a night and make it date night. I take myself out and enjoy my own company. I rise early and take care of duties a husband might be responsible for right now.

I tithe faithfully right now, so any woman who desires to be my wife must know this is what I do. I try and live my life according to the dictates of God. These are just some of the things I do NOW to prepare myself. I am by no means trying to come off as perfect, but I like Paul am striving for it with all my heart, soul, and strength.

As singles we cannot do everything, but don't let that be an excuse to do nothing. If we really do a self-analysis of our lives we will truly find that there are many areas we can sharpen. One of the most important areas we can focus on is being proactive. That means taking personal responsibility for our own actions and behavior. The Bible says, "If ye judge yourself ye need not be judged." There's your secular view and God's Word. This is going to require a cognitive change in one's life.

HANDLING CHANGE

The most productive way to deal with change is to create it. When you actively participate in the changes life brings, there is a better chance of embracing, handling, and sometimes controlling what happens once you participate in creating the change. I honestly feel that if we are willing to have an intimate hand in the inevitable changes in our lives we can learn to deal with them in a more advantageous fashion.

The Bible says that during Paul's conversion on the road to Damascus he experienced a metamorphosis that was completely and totally unexpected (Acts Chapter 9). Have you ever wondered what would have happened if Paul had not been open to God's calling. Thank God Paul refused to refuse. He accepted the call God had on his life and thus became a willing participant in serving God and walking in the purpose God had for his life. Listen my brethren, the truth of the matter is Jesus is coming back to claim his people. Regardless of what any other religions may say.

And he is coming back much sooner than you think. It would behoove every man who has not accepted Jesus as Lord of his life to make that conversion. I beseech thee to give your life to Christ and give it to him yesterday.

I am living proof that regardless of what you may be going through or what you have gone through you are not to far away from the mighty hand of God to be pulled in. Reading this book or any other book man writes will not do us any good without Jesus.

I am sure we all have had times in which we have felt that we should not be here. Times when we felt we should have been dead and gone but God was there. What I've realized after years of escaping the jaws of death is that God didn't just save me from dying but he refused to allow me to die without being saved.

The God we serve is a merciful and forgiving God who wants all his children to make a conscious decision to accept him. His plan is for his children to receive the gift of salvation and begin to walk in the plan and purpose he has for their lives.

Whether you have been a fornicator, drug abuser, alcoholic, or murderer, you can have the unfailing and enduring hand of God reach down and resurrect your life. Because of his Love and Grace I am able to share my experience through the words God placed in my heart.

HEART OF A SINNER

For I Desire Only the Kingdom of Heaven, I Desire Not, The Things of This World. Because I Desire Nothing of This World God Blesses Me With My Heart's Desires. I Am A Righteous Child of God, I Am Not A Sinner, I Am Redeemed, Not Condemned, I Am Saved, Not Lost, I Am Abundantly Blessed, Not Hopelessly Destroyed, Through His Grace I Am Rich Beyond Knowledge. For My Enemies Evil And Wicked Ways Are As Deep As Their Imagination And Their Imagination Is Endless. However, My Lord And Savior Jesus Showers Me And Protects Me With His Infinite Love And Strength In Which Man Cannot Possibly Compare. My Hopes And Prayers Lie At The Feet Of My Heavenly Father. He Hears Me Day And Night With My Constant Calls. He Soothes My Mind And Spirit And Comforts Me For Battle. His Strength Abides In Me And My Obedience, Trust, And Love Is Never Ending. Glory To God. Amen.

When God through his mercy and righteousness pulled me out of the darkness and into his marvelous light I knew in my spirit that saying yes to submitting my life to him meant saying yes to many things. It meant I was willing to lose friends for him. It meant I was willing to lose family members for him. It meant I was willing to give up a many nouns (Persons, Places, Things). That's right my brethren when you come to Christ you are saying I am willing to give up many things in my former life.

This by no means will be an easy task. This will be a laborious and arduous journey but it will be a trek you will never regret. It will be more comforting than your previous life peregrination because you will forever be in the awesome presence of God. That alone is worth shouting about. Glory be to God. *And if God be for you who can be against you?*

It is one thing to be in the lion's den but it is a whole other story to be in a den of lions. A lion's den can be owned by lions, yet empty. A den of lions is fully occupied and extremely dangerous. When we were non-Christians living our lives being driven by our flesh are then *quickened and made alive* through the grace of God, we are now protected regardless of the situation we may find ourselves in. Do not be discouraged while waiting on the LORD. As I have repeated many times, "It came to pass," it didn't come to stay.

TEN THINGS WE CAN DO WHILE PATIENTLY WAITING ON GOD TO BLESS US WITH A MATE:

- Seek God Daily Through Prayer And Biblical Study.
- Meditate On Your Strengths.
- Keep Your Flaws In Perspective. Don't Dwell On Them.
- Focus On Your Potential As A Husband/Wife And What You Offer.
- Never Compare Yourself With Other Singles Or Married People.
- Learn From Your Past Relationships, Good And Bad.
- Accept The Fact That You And Your Mate Will Not Be Perfect.
- Be Yourself.
- Look For Different Ways To Grow Socially.

- Expect God To Bless You With Your Mate At Any Time.

Let's take a look at some of these from biblical and practical view. That's not to say the Bible is not practical so we'll call it the human viewpoint. Studying God's word and developing your prayer life are the two most important things a Christian can do. Single or married it makes no difference.

It amazes me the people who profess they believe in the God of the Bible, but won't study the Bible of the God. Hear me when I say this and never forget what I'm about to say. God loving people do not find time for God's word but they make time. God commands not suggest that we study his life changing Word.

Study (Be Diligent) to show (present) thyself approved unto God, a workman that Needeth not to be ashamed, rightly dividing the word of truth. But shun profane And vain (worthless talk) babblings: for they will increase unto more ungodliness. (2 Timothy 2:15-16)

I have found that this keeps me focused on God and not me. It is important that we never become so obsessed with finding a mate or having a mate find us we forget that God must be first in our lives. I know many people who once they found a mate began to forsake God, and completely forgot is was HIM who blessed them with that particular person in the first place.

We have to be well prepared in spiritual truths regarding how we should govern our lives while waiting on our mate. It is important to understand that society will do everything and anything it can to desensitize Christians to accept their ways and behavior as normal. Though it may be contrary to the Word of God they will try and force-feed us every one of their empty ideas.

It is our responsibility to infect the world with godly behavior rather than allow the lust and impurities of the world to infect us. How do we begin to do that? It all begins with LOVE. The unconditional love of God that he shed abroad in our hearts when he saved us. When people see how we conduct ourselves during our period of singleness it can do nothing but produce a positive response. This response may come from only one person but remember God and one is a majority.

Second, we can focus on the talents God has blessed us with. When God saves us out of darkness and brings us into his marvelous light this should provoke a desire to serve him with our time, talents, and treasure. See God is either LORD of ALL or he's not LORD at ALL.

Therefore, serving God by proclaiming the glorious gospel of Jesus Christ is the greatest form of appreciation a Christian can display. This is not only serving God on Sunday mornings in the House of Prayer, but in ALL facets of our lives. Serving him may consist of going back to school and being a beacon of light in a classroom setting. It may be taking on a part-time job where your godly values can be visibly displayed. You may want to volunteer in the community in some capacity. Thereby, opening up the door to witness about Jesus to the unsaved.

It is amazing to me how many people have come to Jesus only to see what they can get rather than what they can give. When I look back over my life and I think about what he saved me from and what he brought me through, I view it as a privilege and an honor to serve him in whatever capacity he desires.

TEND TO THE ROOTS

If you do some research you will find that most people who have become successful and amassed materialistic wealth in the form of money, homes, property, cars, or business never sought those things. They focused on their talent and how they could become the best with that talent. The possessions ended up being the bi-product of the hard work put in their talent.

If you sit down and talk to Tiger Woods, Michael Jordan, Warren Buffett, Bill Gates, Denzel Washington, or Michael Dell they will tell you they never strived for materialistic things. They focused on the talents God gave them and all those things (materialistic) were added unto them. Now whether or not *they believe* God blessed them with the talent is something only God knows.

However, the Bible says every good and perfect gift comes from God so I know it even if they don't. See I believe the word of God and what it promises so that eliminates any need to manipulate people to get ahead. God says plainly in his word what we can expect when we do things his way. The blessings that God has for his people are systematically connected with their relationship to the Bible. If one truly has faith in Almighty God to bring forth all the blessings that God has promised, then the person will seek to achieve those promises through the only means he has.

Blessed is the man that walketh not in the counsel of the ungodly, nor standeth in the Way of sinners, nor sitteth in the seat of the scornful. But his delight is in the Law of the LORD; and in his Law doth he meditate day and night. And he shall be like a tree Planted by the rivers of water, that bringeth forth his fruit in his season; his leaf also shall Not wither; and whatsoever he doeth shall prosper. (Psalm 1:1-3)

One of the problems amongst God's people is many don't want to delight themselves in his law but want to be blessed with his fruit. God is not in the business of blessing people who are going to turn around and embarrass him. He is looking for people who spend time with him and seek the plan he has for their life and then act on what they believe.

When you neglect to meditate on God's word you find yourself walking not in the counsel of the godly. You then find yourself standing, hanging and fellowshipping with the sinners. This will lead to you becoming infected instead of being the one who is doing the infecting. And when this occurs, a life of willful sin and disobedience is sure to follow. Now, know God will not give up on you but your life will be as fruitless as a withered tree.

And don't think because you don't see the tree of your life wither immediately God has winked at your sin. Know for a surety that God does not settle all his accounts on the first and fifteenth of the month. The children of Israel walked in the wilderness for forty years dying a slow death. I have learned through living and watching people that the anticipation of death is worst than death itself. For forty years people walked around still under the protection of God but knowing the promise land would be something they would never see. How sad!

Hone your talent but don't become obsessed with the fruit that comes from developing your talent. Stay God focused and wilderness death shall surely pass from you. I was reading a personal finance magazine while relaxing in my hotel suite and came across an article which talked about found money.

It said that state coffers held more than $22 billion in unclaimed assets, including lost bank accounts, misplaced bonds and securities, un-cashed dividend checks, uncollected utility deposits and unclaimed life-insurance benefits. I found that quite interesting to say the least. It is ironic that a country that focuses so much on money and materialistic possessions would have that much un-claimed wealth.

This is a perfect example of why it so much more satisfying when you seek Jesus and through seeking HIM you allow your life to be rooted in modesty. The more you have the more time and attention you have to allocate to watching over it. Eventually, something is going to come up lost or misappropriated. Therefore, focus on serving the LORD and he will supply ALL your needs according to his riches in glory.

Third, NEVER give too much credence to your flaws or past failures. I am not saying you should not remember them; please do. However, this should be done for the sole purpose of learning but be able to develop a spiritual quality I call "Spiritual Amnesia."

That is to say remember the potholes you hit during this journey called LIFE, but be able to forget them just the same. Another example would be that when you do something you consider nice for someone you should immediately forget it, but if someone does something nice for you, ALWAYS remember it.

You know Christians today are smarter than they have ever been about things that simply have no value regarding the destiny God has for their life. Because of this many people focus on what they don't have or what they haven't done and lose valuable time concerning themselves with what went wrong rather than what can go right.

Be careful (anxious)(worried) for nothing; but in EVERY thing by PRAYER and SUPPLICATION with THANKSGIVING Let your request be made know unto God. And the PEACE of GOD, which surpasseth all understanding, shall keep (guard) Your HEARTS and MINDS through Christ Jesus. (Philippians 4:6-7)

See there is no reason to be concerned with the past except to learn. The secular world has a saying that says those who don't remember their past are doom to repeat it. God addressed it in his Word well before they thought it. Christians must ALWAYS remember God covers all aspects of life in his precious Word.

I have learned that to worry about the past is simply useless. The reason is because when we worry what we do is remove God from the equation. We unconsciously say I have to do something to rectify what went wrong but I don't know what. This produces worry. Worry usually involves past failures, present calamity, or future expectations. Listen if you can't change the past, present, or future then don't worry about it. If you can then just do it. If you have failed in relationships in the past ask God to show you where you went wrong and move on.

The worst thing you can do is drag that past into your present. And if you don't cut it off from your present it is sure to end up bleeding into your future. I remember praying to God to fill me with the Spirit so I could develop my ability to LOVE unconditionally. Let me tell you something. If you cannot open up to God you will never be able to open up to people. And if you cannot open up to people you are not ready for a mate. Therefore, we should always seek God to help us to be real and truthful with ourselves.

I was finding myself meeting women, courting women, and then when I found out some minute thing I didn't like, I intentionally found a way to sabotage the relationship. I knew I could not continue this behavior and only God could change this because I could not. One of my favorite scriptures is at the end of John 15:5 when our LORD Jesus says, "For Without Me Ye Can Do Nothing." This is something EVERY living person needs to know.

Finally, single men and women must make a cognitive effort to just be who God has made you to be. In this world where following the Jones' is an ever increasingly popular theme we have to remain steadfast in being ourselves. We must make up our mind that we need not be a cheap copy but a godly original. Lest see what God says about changing our attitudes and minds and following the cues of the world.

For of HIM, and Through HIM, and To HIM, are ALL things: to whom be glory for Ever. AMEN. I Beseech you Therefore, brethren, by the mercies of God, that YE PRESENT Your bodies a living sacrifice, holy, acceptable unto God, which is your Reasonable(spiritual)(rational) service. And be not Conformed to THIS world: BUT be Ye transformed by the RENEWING of YOUR MIND, that ye may prove what is that Good and Acceptable and Perfect will of God. (Romans 11:36, 12:1-2)

As single Christians we have to make changes in the way we think because how we think will affect how we act. At the end of the day does it really matter what people think about you? Does it matter what your standing is in society? Is it noteworthy that you are popular are not? The only opinion that should matter to a Christian is the opinion of God's. What does God think of me? If you allow that to be your life's theme everything will inevitably fall into place.

STAND YOUR GROUND

Let me share something with you about being confident in yourself. I'm talking about godly confidence and not worldly arrogance. I have been in the midst of wealthy athletes, musicians, actors, actresses, and CEOs. Now here I am in the company of these people discussing a myriad of things. And as I stand there talking to the world's elite I am keenly aware that they decorated with thousand dollar suits, thousand dollar dresses, shoes worth hundreds of dollars, and enough jewelry to possibly pay my salary for a year or two.

I stand there in a three-figure suit, a twenty-dollar shirt, and a pair of two hundred dollar shoes and one piece of jewelry (Watch) and the price of what we are wearing is never becomes a topic. I'm never asked who my tailor is. I never ask who is your tailor. I never ask where you purchased your shoes neither am I asked where my shoes were purchased. Compliments may exchange regarding our attire but that is the extent of it.

What's most interesting is regardless of the difference in our salaries I am able to stand right there and hold my own regardless of the subject or topic of conversation. As a matter of fact because of the wisdom of God, I find that I am sometimes the most astute joker in the bunch. See my point is when you spend time kneeling before God you can stand before ANY man. You will also find out that when you are around many wealthy people money doesn't drive them. It is not only because they already have it. It is because now that they have it they realize they do have money it ceases to motivate them.

This is why I can honestly say I have never and never will ask another human being for his or her autograph. Now I know you should never say never but for the life of me I have not figured out what the purpose of that is all about. I understand someone signing a personal work they have been blessed to do such as a book, magazine, or Compact Disc, but to have someone sign a piece of paper is mind boggling to say the least.

Another thing I have found to be helpful is to make list of the qualities you expect your future spouse to have. Do a compare and contrast and complete a mock interview with yourself. Please do not say you don't know what you want in a man or woman. I know my future wife must be a God-fearing woman with values that are similar to my mother. I didn't say I was looking for a mother figure but someone with the drive and determination my mother possessed. My mother's character was impeccable. She displayed the strength that a woman must display in order to become my wife. This is one of the qualities my future wife must possess.

If you don't know what you want you could end up with something you don't want. It that's simple. This is why many people get frustrated while waiting on the LORD. They really don't know what they are waiting for. God could send the perfect person into his or her life and it not be known. This is why it is vital to make a physical or at least mental note as to what you are expecting God to give you in a mate.

Another thing I do while waiting on the LORD is exercise my body. The Bible says, "Bodily exercise profiteth little but godliness is profitable unto all things." (1 Timothy 4:8). Now it says it profiteth little but it didn't say it profiteth nothing. You would think it says nothing by the way many people take care of themselves. Your body is the temple of the Holy Spirit and you want to do anything you can protect that temple. There are consequences to not paying attention to your physical body. Remember John 10:10 says, "The thief cometh not, but for to steal, and to kill, and to destroy: I am come that they might have life, and that they might have it more abundantly."

You must know the devil doesn't care how he short-circuits your life. He'll use sexual temptation, lust for money, or even gluttony to destroy your life. Being single allows you the opportunity to focus on God and then focus on you. Bodily exercise could be the habit that makes the difference between in how long you may be around.

It profiteth little not profiteth nothing. Take care of your whole self. Listen to what Paul says in 1 Thessalonians 5:23, "And the very God of peace sanctify you wholly; and I pray God your whole Spirit and Soul and Body be preserved blameless unto the coming of our LORD Jesus Christ."

You see that? Paul prays that your whole Spirit, Soul, and Body be preserved blameless unto the coming of our LORD. This is clear and precise proof God expects us to exercise all three. We are made in the image of God and God is expressed in three persons: God the Father, The Son, and The Holy Spirit. We have Spirit, Soul, and Body.

Therefore, we must habitually exercise them all. Satan will attack us from all angles and our body is not off limits to his attack. This brings to mind many Christians who have gone on to be with the lord at what we consider a young age. And in many instances their physical health played a major role in their early demise.

There were things they could have done to extend their life and chose not to do it. These consist of the refraining from smoking, overeating, drinking, and laziness. Christians do engage in these things and I beseech all the brethren to pray for those we know are still struggling in these areas. Understand exercising your body not only helps your overall health, but it has been known to relieve stress, increase energy, and saves you money. Yes, saves you money!

I have known people who by letting themselves go physically, outgrew their entire wardrobes, and were forced to spend money for clothes they did not have. In many instances the money spent was not in the budget and caused other financial problems.

And here lies some of the problems many Christians endure unnecessarily. We allow one problem to bleed into another area in our life and open up another avenue for the enemy to step in. Listen, the Bible says we are required to be faithful stewards over the money, time, and gifts God has blessed us with. And when you spend time with God he will open you up to so much knowledge you cannot help but increase in materialistic blessings.

INNER GROWTH

We should always be exercising our spirit man. This should be the number one muscle we build up. The way to fend off the urges to become entangled with the cares of this world is to build up our spirit man. Paul says we are to be filled with spirit. This filling comes after being indwelt by the spirit.

...the fruit of the Spirit is Love, Joy, Peace, Long-Suffering, Gentleness, Goodness, Faith, Meekness, Temparance against such there is no law. (Galatians 5:22-23)

When we are "born again" we are indwelt by the Holy Spirit. When we continue to prayer, study and fellowship with other Christians it should lead to spiritual growth. When spiritual growth occurs there should be evidence of our rebirth. This is what Jesus meant when he said, "You will know a tree by its fruit."

These are the characteristics of a spirit-filled Christian. There are many debates in denominations regarding the spiritual gifts. So you will have professing Christians with nasty attitudes claiming they have the gift of tongues. You have hateful Christians claiming they have the gift of interpretation of tongues. You have prideful Christians claiming the gift of healing.

We argue and bicker over these things from New York to California and the whole time neglect what most important aspect of a Christian's life should be. That is *The Fruit of the Spirit.* While waiting on the LORD we need to seriously seek him to find out where are we requiring the most improvement of these nine components that make up the fruit.

This is the essence of what makes a sound Christian. Individually each one has incomparable value but together they form a formidable team. An all-star cast that would make any Christian who allows this fruit to flow, a powerful witness for the LORD Jesus Christ.

The fruit of Love allows each Christian the strength to love God and God's people. The Ten Commandments are divided into two categories. The first tablet speaks about man and his love and relationship to God. The second tablet speaks of man's relationship to man. Both of these are vitally important and cannot be separated. Remember Paul nestled the Love Chapter (Number Thirteen in the Book of Corinthians) right between two chapters focusing on gifts of the Spirit. Carnal people and congregations focus on the gifts more than the fruit. This ought not to be so!

When the rich young ruler approached Jesus about inheriting eternal life Jesus pointed to the second tablet of the Ten Commandments (Read Gospel of Mark Chapter Ten). The rich ruler stated that he had done all of those things from his youth. If you notice when reading you see that Jesus didn't even dispute this claim.

Nevertheless, Jesus pointed to one thing he lacked and commanded him to sell all his goods and give them to the poor. The Bible says he went away grieved for he had many possessions (his possessions had him). He had religion but no relationship.

He came running and even kneeled at the feet of Jesus, but that was pure religion and when Jesus requested relationship he turned and walked away. Jesus wants to bless us in ways we have not even begun to imagine. Ephesians 3:20 states, "Jesus is able to do exceeding abundantly above all that we ask or think, according to the power that worketh in us."

The end of this verse says according to the power that worketh in us because we must seek a relationship with Jesus at all cost. Simple religion is vain and empty and without relationship is simply useless. I honestly believe that if you remove sacrificial offerings, freewill offerings, tithing, love gifts, first fruits, or just money period from many churches in America, most pastors wouldn't even bother showing up.

Money has become such a problem in the American pulpit that many of the unsaved simply refuse to come to. The problem is those in the pulpit cannot and refuse to see this is a problem. Modesty has taken a quick exit and our preachers are seeking to live more like celebrities than the celebrities actually are. When this attitude is made mention of the cry of jealousy occurs. But why would anyone think Christian folk are jealous about this?

Christians are out there trying to let the rich and famous know they need Jesus. And the preachers are trying to be rich and famous. You can't get a more mixed message than this. We are not jealous but we are sick and tired of having to defend some of the nonsense that goes on in God's house. The credibility of the church is paramount and the leaders are the biggest culprits of destroying that credibility. God wants all his children to be prosperous but never at the expense of his eternal plan. We should never be off doing our own thing for selfish gain. Our lifestyle should reflect a godly modesty the sinner could envy.

Relationship with Jesus must always be the foundation of the church and its people if we are ever going to continue to win souls. Don't get me wrong because God can go right around every preacher in the world and get the job done. But if people truly feel God has called them to preach then just preach. Dispense with the circus that is encircling many American pulpits.

It only opens a hole for Satan to come through and believe me he doesn't need much. Vanity and self-aggrandizement must be eradicated from all Christian lives or there will be many lives lost to the devil unnecessarily.

Now back to the man who walked away from Jesus. The Bible says he was a RICH, YOUNG, RULER. He had money, prestige, popularity, and power, yet in the depths of his soul he KNEW he had no relationship. Yet, when given a choice between doing things the world's way and God's way he made a decision that would ultimately bring death.

Second, of the Fruit, is the Joy that comes from knowing the Savior has redeemed us. This joy is not moved or swayed regardless of the vicissitudes of life. Paul would say in Philippians 4:12, "I know both how to be abased and I know how to abound: every where and in ALL things I am instructed both to be full and to be hungry, both to abound and to suffer need."

This is the joy that a Christian rooted with this fruit should exude on a consistent basis. One must remember Paul wrote this epistle while in prison. Paul knew like we know that as we wait on the LORD we may feel like we are suffering but through it ALL God will accomplish a good that will bring HIM glory.

That is what our lives and relationships should bring and that is glory to God. The Bible says we were created for HIS pleasure and He takes pleasure in the prosperity of his people. This is important to understand so you won't get bitter when trials come. I said when trials come because they will be coming. But they come to make us better.

Third, is Peace that comes from the security of knowing we are God's children forever. This is peace that allows one to turn a blind eye to ridicule and persecution. We have peace with God and the peace of God. These here my brethren is a powerful duo. This is so important that Jesus takes time to remind us through his Word.

Peace I leave with you, my peace I give unto you: not as the world giveth, give I unto You. Let not your heart be troubled, neither let it be afraid. (John 14:27)

Hallelujah. Hallelujah. Hallelujah. Paul would later add that the peace of God that surpasses all understanding is able to guard our heart and mind. I remind you he was able to write this while in prison. Be aware that any attack that you may endure will come many times to drive you crazy. You will see many friends in wonderful relationships and wonder what in the world is wrong with me. Be not dismayed because if you do not faint you shall reap.

Fourth, is the Long-Suffering that is needed when loneliness starts applying pressure to the human mind. Let me finish my thought from my peace description with a powerful scripture. Galatians 6:9 says, "Let us not be weary in well doing: for in DUE season we shall reap, IF we faint (do not lose heart) not."

God says there will be seasons we must go through that will test us to our limits. We will be pushed to the brink of giving up. Please do not lose heart for our labor will not be in vain. This is much easier to say than to do. I can truly attest to that. But God is rich in mercy and will not allow us to suffer more than we can stand.

Fifth, is the Gentleness that translates into being kind to all of God's people including ourselves. I know you would think that goes without saying, but many people are seeking a spouse and do not know how to be treat themselves. Practice being kind to yourself and fulfill the rumor that states old habits are hard to break. Get in the habit of treating yourself with gentleness so it will become natural when your mate comes.

Sixth, is the Goodness that translates in being generous to all those you may meet. Remember everything you have comes from God. It does not matter how blessed we become God expects us to remember those who are less fortunate. Any surplus of anything we have that is deemed good should be shared with those who are less fortunate. God says when we give and shall be given back to us. This is why it makes no sense for Christians to display an attitude of greed. We could never out-give God and it pleases him when we take time to bless another. We open up a conduit for God to bless us with whatever blessings he would like us have. This is a quality every single Christian better perfect because this is pivotal when developing a relationship.

The world will not lay down many examples for the Christian family to follow in the giving department. Giving is part of the necessary foundation for any type of godly union. The Christian's ability to give willing in any area shows the willingness to give period. Therefore, if a person enters into a relationship that gift of giving has a better opportunity to surface. By the same token if one doesn't have the propensity to want to share there will be problems in any team. God has richly blessed us and did through the gift of giving and expects us to follow his lead in every thing we do. We are to delete snobbery from our lives and bless all those we are in the position to bless. God says it best in the following scriptures.

Charge them that are rich in this world, that they be not high-minded, nor trust In uncertain riches, but in the living God, who giveth us richly all things to enjoy; That they do good, that they be rich in good works, ready to distribute, willing to Communicate (share); Laying up in store for themselves a good foundation against The time to come, that they may lay hold on eternal life. (1 Timothy 6:17-19)

Seventh, is the Faith that we have that will remain unmovable and steadfast in the hope we have attained in Christ Jesus. Not a hope of wishing something happens but an expectant hope of knowing something is coming. Faith that bleeds faithfulness and dependability to stand up for God regardless what the opposition brings.

When sexual lusts come faith says back off. When an affair with a married man or woman presents itself faith says I'll wait on Jesus. When the opportunity to make a little extra money in an immoral way rears its ugly head faith says God shall supply all my needs according to his riches. Unmovable.

Eighth, is showing Meekness in troubling times. Understand meekness that is the opposite of weakness. Meekness is controlled strength. Meekness is not using your power when you could. Meekness is refusing to flex and conceding for the glory of God. Meekness is being falsely accused and never saying a word.

Meekness is being scourged and whipped and not dying on the post. Hallelujah. Meekness is carrying the cross up Calvary for the World. Praise the LORD. Meekness is hanging on the cross when you could have summoned Legions of Angels to destroy us all. Meekness is JESUS.

Ninth, is the Temperance that manifest self-control. When lusts and passions from old spring up in your mind send temperance to the rescue. When that old lover calls for a one-night stand send temperance to the rescue. When something untouchable is placed in your midst send temperance to the rescue. When you feel like you are about to burst within send temperance to the rescue.

Nine components of the "Fruit of the Spirit" working in harmony to show forth the glory of God in a Christian's life. Every Christian may not have the same level of fruit but every Christian should have some fruit. Jesus when giving a parable regarding the seed said some brought forth fruit, some a hundredfold, some sixty-fold, and some thirty-fold. Nevertheless, all ground that is the HEART when sowed by seed that is the WORD should bring forth fruit. This is the EVIDENCE that one has been washed in the blood of Jesus Christ.

My beloved let he that hath an ear hear what the spirit saith to the churches.

FIVE
EXPECTATIONS

*My Soul Wait Thou Only Upon
God; For My Expectation is From Him.* (PSALM 62:5)

I purposely placed this chapter directly behind the waiting on the LORD chapter because as we are waiting on God to bless us with a lifelong companion I feel it is necessary we have some expectation of what we want God to send.

The bible says in Proverbs 18:22, "Whoso findeth a wife findeth a good thing, and obtaineth favor of the LORD." So we do have a scripture from the Word of God regarding who should be finding and who should be looking to be found. I thought the women might need to know this.

Now notice what I said. Men should be finding a good wife. Men should be the hunters and not the hunted. We should be taking the role of leadership. The Holy Spirit should be actively leading the man in the pursuit of a godly wife. He should not be using the world's script but spiritual discernment to put him in the correct place.

Also, I said women should be expecting to be found. Place close attention to the words I used. Women though not finding should be expecting. I don't mean to be ambiguous in my wording but you must understand something. It is a myth that women should be sitting on the porch or just relaxing near a brook not looking for her future mate to show up. On the contrary, both men and women who have a desire in their heart for marriage should have an elevated sense of expectation.

I said earlier that men should not be using the secular methods to find his wife. When I say this I speaking of the places that have no evidence of harboring women who may have a relationship with God. I will not go into naming these places but many Christian singles are being found in some of these ungodly environments.

Someone once said "I looked for the church and found it in the world and I looked for the world and found it in the church." This statement unfortunately is dripping with truth. I'm not talking about sinners coming to the House of Prayer with the expectation of coming to Christ. I live for these miracle works wrought by God. I am talking about what and where single Christians are spending time.

I don't know if you noticed but I did not use the phrase free time because Christians must understand there is no such thing as free time. Jesus Christ paid an enormous price for every single second of every single minute of every single hour of every single day of every single week of every single month of every single year of our lives.

We are always on display and never more than when we are away from God's house. I distinctly remember during a time of backsliding that I would always be carousing at various nightclubs and bars. It seemed like the best place for me to be. Now what is interesting is when I came back to Jesus I began serving in the church I noticed something interesting. While spending as much time there as I could in church I was quite surprised at what I saw.

The more time I spent at the church the more people I began to meet and see. That wasn't what I found surprising. I began to notice that there were countless people I would recognize from the same bars and nightclubs in which I had just left. I assumed that they like myself were turning over a new leaf and deciding to allow Jesus to be LORD of their life.

I found this to be quite the opposite. Most if not all of the people I had noticed had been attending and professing to be Christians for years. After conversing with them I would find out that they had been saved for extended periods of time. I found this interesting to say the least. I never let them know that I had just noticed them the prior week at these places.

But believe I would have never thought I would find Christians there. I say this to say that had I been a weak Christian this could have provoked me to think I could go right back into those environments. I would have thought it would have been just fine to be in a local dive on Saturday night and ushering in the church at six o'clock Sunday morning.

I thank God for convicting me at the mere thought of such nonsense. See my beloved as we patiently wait on the LORD we must rid ourselves of these old sinful habits and let God replace them with new and improved proclivities. We NEVER know who is watching or what type of impact our actions can have. We are not in darkness anymore and must separate ourselves from the unfruitful works of darkness.

A PREPARED PLACE

Let's take a look and where we were and where we must go to allow God to get us in the place we need to be. God tells us something about ourselves that may be hard to believe but God cannot lie.

And you hath he quickened (made alive), who were dead in trespasses and sins; Wherein in time past ye walked according to the course (age) of this world, according To the prince of the power of the air, the spirit that now worketh in the children of Disobedience: Among whom also we all had (conducted ourselves) our conversation in Times past in the lusts of our flesh, fulfilling the desires of the flesh and of the mind; and Were by nature the children of wrath, even as others. (Ephesians 2:1-3)

Can you believe that? God is talking about what we used to be. He's talking about what we used to do. He's pointing out what we used seek. I said used to be, do, and seek. However, verse number four starts with two words that immediately change our position.

BUT GOD! That is all it takes to change a sinner's position in life. The Bible states that by our born human nature we were not even thinking about doing what God would have us to do. Reading this should inspire every Christian to want to live the rest of their life as a disciple for Jesus Christ. People don't even know the light is off. They are just doing what comes natural before meeting Christ.

But when you confess to be a Christian you are not in that group anymore. This has somehow been misplaced in the mind of the Christian. You should not be doing the same things you were doing prior to coming to Christ. This is important because we should be spending the rest of our lives knowing, loving, and serving the LORD Jesus Christ.

Our expectations from a mate should not come from the cesspool of worldly and ungodly people. Just pick up a newspaper any morning and you will see the ungodly are the last people we should be following. They have made a mockery of relationships and marriage through sitcoms and reality TV. It is a shame to see the examples the young people in this country have been given. Is it a wonder why teenage pregnancy and fatherless homes are rapidly increasing. I know that sounds strong but let me give you scripture so you won't put the book down in a fit of anger.

Be ye not unequally yoked together with unbelievers: for what fellowship (in common) Hath righteousness with unrighteousness? And what communion (fellowship) hath light With darkness? Where fore come out from among them, and be ye separate said the LORD, and touch not the unclean thing; and I will receive you, and will be a father unto You, and ye shall be my sons and daughters, saith the LORD Almighty. Having Therefore these promises, dearly beloved, let us cleanse ourselves from all filthiness of the flesh and spirit, perfecting HOLINESS in the fear of God. (2 Corinthians 6:14, 17-18, 7:1)

...have NO fellowship with the unfruitful works of darkness, but rather reprove them. (Ephesians 5:11)

Now there is written proof that I'm not just spouting off my own opinion. This is clear evidence regarding with whom and where we should spending our time.

HURTFUL COMPROMISE

I was reading a popular Christian magazine and came across an article discussing shackin'. For those of you who have decided to use that gift of spiritual amnesia let me explain. Shackin' is the secular or street term given for a man and woman who are not married yet are cohabitating together. They are not married but are living as if they were. Simple and to the quick. Shackin', Shackin', Shackin'.

What was interesting is there were a host of facts and figures noting the negative outlook shackin' had on the couple's future marriage. The numbers as expected were not favorable. But that's not what I found puzzling. The pastor explaining the behavior came to the conclusion that rather than call this lifestyle of sin disobedience to God, we should re-define it for the sinner's sake. He felt we should remove the religious stigma and see the unbelieving world as people struggling to make life work without the Bible.

This is why our churches are experiencing the problems they are. This is exactly what Satan hopes we do. He hopes we change the standards of God. If you are going to elevate man righteousness you must re-define and reduce sin. Now I am beginning to understand why the church is becoming a laughingstock. And remember this was a pastor making this statement.

Let me tell all of you something right now. God calls this behavior sin. Sin is missing the mark. Not missing it as someone who is aiming and trying to hit it, but someone who is deliberately disobeying God, his Holy character and thus missing it intentionally. Now if people who say they have been called to preach the wonderful Gospel of Jesus Christ won't call it what it is then why would the very people they lead do it. Beloved, highlight this so you'll always know where it is. Jesus Christ did not die to give us a better personality, a house, a car, a husband, a wife, a job, a degree, a family or to keep us from struggling.

As a matter of fact I have struggled more since coming to Jesus than before. Our LORD himself said that there would be persecution to endure in this lifetime and as usual was right.

The pastor went on to develop an understanding of why the people were shackin'. Well, if he would have picked up the very Bible I hope he reads, studies, and preaches from, he could found the answer in the aforementioned scriptures in Ephesians. Yet, rather than introduce them to Jesus explain to them that without Christ they are destined for eternal separation from God he devised a plan to provide for them a free wedding.

People, a marriage and a wedding are two entirely different things and as we patiently wait on the LORD we better make sure we understand that. If two sinners come together and with the pageantry of a beauty contest engage in the covenant of God's holy institution you have done exactly one thing. You have married two unrepentant sinners. You have done more harm than hurt for where was the confession of sin against God? Where was the repentance which needed to come from each person's own heart? Where was the acceptance of Jesus Christ as savior?

Instead of introducing Christ we are introducing a new way to the promises of Christ. Some of you may say well now that they married maybe they will give their lives to Christ. They could very well happen but what if they don't. The Gospel is not a mechanism in which we invite me people to come to the church to receive blessings from God.

The Gospel is what the entire creation hinges upon. The invitation is to accept Christ as savior and be saved. Saved from what? Eternal condemnation and separation from God. It doesn't matter whether you are rich, broke, single, black, white, short, tall, democrat, or republican.

NOT OUR WAY

Listen as a Christian we should feed the hungry, clothed the naked, engage in humanitarian efforts, and partake in philanthropy. But, we cannot flip do those things and think it makes us a Christian. The contemporary church has in so many instances decided to putt the cart before the horse. We are inviting the people to everything but Jesus.

Is your marriage a wreck? Come on down. Are you shackin'? Come on down. Are you out of work? Come on down. You need a miracle in your life? Come on down. Let me tell you something you may not know. You can with all sincerity take a walk down any church isle and prostrate yourself on the altar and repent. If you get up having truly given your life to Jesus, you can walk right back to your seat and months or years later lose your wife, lose your job and find yourself experiencing deathly sickness.

What Jesus promises is that regardless of what life throws you HE will never leave you nor forsake you and he will give you peace and comfort in your life to bear it all. He will allow you to rise every day and witness to someone else about HIM. He will introduce you to your new best friends: GRACE and MERCY. And as you grow in him you will find that all those external things will cease to matter.

...though our outward man perish, yet the inward man is renewed day by day, For our Light affliction which is but for a moment, worketh for us a far more exceeding and Eternal weight of glory; While we look not at the things which are seen, but at the things which are not seen: for the things which are seen are temporal; but he things which are Not seen are eternal. (2 Corinthians 4:16-18)

See when you live and preach the gospel the way Jesus, John the Baptist, Peter, and Paul preached and live you won't be all that popular. That's why it's important to know that just because you see big crowds that doesn't mean the gospel is being taught.

It is much more profitable to tell people what they want to hear. But this is sadly done at the expense of God's people. Yes God will even the score but in the mean time people are expecting the wrong thing at the wrong time. God has told us that these perilous times shall come. He even says that silly women laden with sins would be lead captive away with divers lusts ever learning, and never able to come to the knowledge of the truth.

God's Bible is the truth but when people have a certain level of expectation they will be willing to believe whatever lines up with their own carnal desires. So Christian men will not seek God's wisdom for what they should expect in a wife. They take the advice from any Johnny come lately who says God has a new way. But God says in Proverbs 14:12, "There is a way which seemeth right unto a MAN; but the end thereof are the ways of death."

HONESTY WORKS

Many people get themselves in a fix and immediately point the finger at Satan. But on so many occasions we devise schemes and tricks on our own which turn out to be self-destructive. It is a fact men are moved by their visual senses. We initially choose women based on their pulchritude. We look for the finest, sexist, most beautiful woman and zero in on her and she only. We salivate over her secular trinity measurements 34-26-34. God steps in and gives numerous signs that should immediately send us scurrying for cover, but we simply can't resist. We know the personalities are not compatible.

She's not a Christian and is not sure if she will be anytime soon. Her entire personality is laced with the pride and arrogance of a prima donna. If you looked in the dictionary for the word pretentious you would see her picture. Christian men see her and take discernment and put it in their hip pocket.

Why do we do it? It appeals to our flesh nature. This is why it is important to increase the power of the spirit man while also learning to control the mind and subdue the flesh. The spirit has to be in control because this is how you will know what God has sent and what the enemy has sent. Do you remember in the Gospel of St. John chapter number four where Jesus has a conversation with a woman at the well of Jacob? She tells Jesus about her fathers or ancestors worshiping in the mountain. Jesus then lets her know that to have any relationship with God the seen must be replaced with the unseen. The terrestrial must be replaced with the celestial. He lets her know that God is Spirit and must be worshipped in Spirit and in Truth. As a matter of fact the Bible says he seeketh such. He tells her what God expects.

When you do an etymological study on the word expectation you get many definitions. It is the act of expecting. It consists of the belief about (or mental picture of) the future or future events. It is the conscious wishing for something with confidence of fulfillment.

It can be the eager anticipation of some event. The prospect of the future that something excellent is expected to happen. It speaks of the feeling that something is about to happen. Wishing with confidence of fulfillment. Now let's move from a study to a pericope. Psalm 62:5 says, "My soul wait thou only upon God; for my expectation is from HIM."

When women are expecting a child there is a metamorphosis they go through internally and externally. Internally there is something birthed in them. That is how you should be expecting your future mate. While God is preparing him he should be preparing you. You should be scaling back where you need to scale back and increase where you need to increase. What are the things you see (with your spiritual eye) that you can do to improve your standing as a wife.

I'll let you in on a secret prayer of mine. When I pray to God regarding a mate I always ask God to show me what I can do be a better husband, father, son, servant, friend, and disciple. Though I am not married I see myself married and am already asking God to show me ways to improve my marital standing.

When women are expecting they eat differently. You can't keep listening to the same advice regarding a mate. When you have purposed it in your heart that the time and season is right for you to settle down you have to guard your gates. These are your eye and ear gates. Take your mind off the world and focus immediately on God. What someone else did may have some experiential benefit but take all advice given by request with a grain of salt. You should be taking your final cues from God.

Women who are expecting begin to walk differently. They change where they walk. They can't walk down the same roads they normally walked down. Those roads worked when you were single and not expecting but that has all changed. You can't walk with the same people you walked with before. If you have been spending significant time with single friends you may want to spend some time with the married ones. Start getting a feel for the things married people experience. You will have to endure your own experiences but it never hurts to hear what other couples are going through. It may change your mind altogether about getting married at that time. Remember a delay does not mean you have been denied.

Now ladies it is important that you have some physical expectations of the man you are expecting God to send. I cannot count the times I have asked women what type of guy they were looking. After asking I hear a laundry list of internal qualities come out of their mouths. But when I asked for the physical attributes that fell into the category of it doesn't matter. Now if this had a hint of truth it would be simply marvelous. But men and women both know this is quite far from the truth. Though men seem to be more interested in the physical attractiveness of the person, woman do not lag too far behind.

Single ladies please quit doing this to your selves. There is nothing wrong with being physically attracted to a certain looking man. If you can believe God for one thing in your life why not believe him in this area of your life. Remember ALL of it is small to him so it's not like God has to really sweat it out to find a way to bring the type of God-fearing man you want in your life. I must give a word of caution here for men and women. Please brace yourself for this shocking piece of bulletin news. We ALL have Flaws. Nobody is PERFECT. You WILL NOT find the PERFECT person. Sorry to burst your bubble. However, there is light at the end of the tunnel.

When God connects you with someone who seems to have the qualities you are looking for (I'm speaking to Men and Women) focus on the strong points. Why, because their strong points may line up perfectly with your weak points and your strong points may line up with their weak points. It does neither party to be connected with someone who is just PERFECT. If this happens there will not be any room to grow. We should look forward to being with someone who allows us to mature and grow as a person. We should want someone to help us understand that relationships are not about he/she having every quality exactly the way we want it. Our relationship with God isn't like that. God looks at us as a piece of marred clay but rather than discard us he allows the Holy Spirit to do its perfect work in our lives.

Nevertheless, we have responsibilities as free will agents in the economy of God. When we refuse to position ourselves for the impending harvest of our labor we increase the chances of failure when our ship comes in. This brings to mind what Paul says in Philippians 2:12-13 when God says to us to, "Work out your own salvation with fear and trembling. For it is God which worketh in you both to will and to do of or according to HIS good pleasure." God wants us involved and not mere spectators as we progress in the growth in all facets of our lives. It does not matter what area in our life we are expecting God to bless. HE wants us to eagerly be working and doing this with the tools and instructions he provides.

Many people assume that marriage will induce a positive change on life's outlook. I have found by talking to many married couples that whatever you are single is what you will bring to the marriage. And there may not be much change during the tenure of the marriage. There is usually a brief emotional high immediately after the wedding.

However, both parties usually return to their normal selves and thus the same outlook on life they had prior to tying the knot. I am sure there are many exceptions to the rule and I truly hope so. I just feel it necessary to give a warning to those who are expecting the institution of marriage to change their outlook on life.

People may be surprised that they will feel no more satisfied than they were before the marriage. What I am trying to say is Christians who are satisfied with their WHOLE life prior to marriage tend to mature as people and stay married longer than those who enter marriage dissatisfied. Single is not just being by one's self. Single in Christ Jesus is being Separated, Unique, and Whole. Hallelujah.

STILL VALUABLE

In the Gospel of St. Luke there are three parables in chapter number fifteen. Each parable tells the story of one lost or missing item. Yet despite the loss of the item the owner never ceases to see value in the item and thus gloried to see the one missing item restored. God sees all singles as valuable commodities. That is why heaven throws a party when one soul is saved. We all are important to Christ.

We are all quite unique and possess gifts and talents he wants us to use. As singles we have more time and treasure to use for to the Glory of God. That will change when and if we get married. This is why we should take advantage of being single. I have found the married want to taste single life again and the single are ready to taste marriage.

While we patiently anticipate what God is preparing for us we should be about God's business like our very lives depend upon it. With esprit de corps we should work diligently to build up the household of faith. We should faithfully labor to help bear up the walls of protection for God's people against all powers and principalities.

We must not forget that Jesus Christ our LORD and Savior spent thirty years preparing for a three and a half year ministry. I believe he had an exalted and elevated expectation for his pre-ordained task. Nevertheless, we study and find out he was a carpenter's (Joseph) son. The Bible says that when Jesus was twelve he tarried behind during a religious feast. After returning and finding Jesus three days later the Bible says Jesus went back and was subject or obeyed his parents. So we see even Jesus stayed busy and kept the commandments of God whereby increasing with wisdom and stature, and in favor with God and man.

Folks if Jesus Christ was subject to his earthly parents how much more should we be subject to our heavenly father. Men I am talking specifically to you now. We have a major role to play in God's providential plans. He has extremely high expectations of us. In the Garden of Eden order was reversed and Eve was feeding her husband instead of Adam feeding his wife. Since then we have had a society that prides itself on women's lib and discarding the order of God. Able body men are using women by sitting on their behinds while women go out and work. If a man is a real man he is going to want to work. He may not have a job because of circumstances out of his control but he wants a job in the worse way. All through the Bible we see wonderful men of God doing mighty works.

We need the wisdom of God to do these works. When we gain the wisdom of God we develop the ability to live life skillfully and thus produce something of quality for God. This must be done habitually. To do something once is not habitual behavior. A job is something we should habitually desire to have. Now you may have non-believing associates who will not think what I am saying makes any sense. But know for a surety one of the biggest schisms in relationships is money.

If you are expecting a queen to find her way into your life you better be able to take care of her like a Man of God should? Yes women are getting degrees and developing careers more than ever but you should see her as unemployed when planning your future. She may want to work but you should always be prepared in the event children are added. Your wife may need to stay home for a while or better yet permanently.

These are scenarios you must visualize. My brethren you are put on notice that women will want you to know about the very things I just mentioned. Do you work, did you go to college, do you save, do you invest, where do you want to be in two, four, seven, ten years? And just because a woman asks those questions, it does not mean that is all she interested in. She is asking the correct questions and I concur one hundred percent. All women are not gold-diggers. If these seem like gold-digging questions then you probably don't have any gold anyway. Men with gold don't mind someone doing a little digging because they're usually anxious to show it.

I have a daughter and I am teaching her now by providing for her in a way she will never forget. As she matures and witnesses what I am doing she will expect any man in her life to meet or beat her earthly father. Any man who is blessed with the opportunity to become her husband will have major shoes to fill. He must first receive approval from her heavenly father and then it gets worse.

Let's compare and contrast what men and women tend to expect from one another. Men tend to want admiration from their mate, while women seek affection. How do both get what they want in a relationship? When the man comes home from a long day at the office his wife should greet him with a word of encouragement. She can affirm the fact that he is appreciated and it would be tragic if he were not the head of the family. The man can let his wife know she is the oil that keeps his engine running and without her the machine simply does not work.

Also, men need intimacy while women want romance. Men take your wife to an elegant restaurant when finances and time permit. Women reward your mate by bringing romance into the home. Middle ground is priceless in a relationship. All of these are not safe-proof but they are suggestions I know have been tested and found true.

In addition, men are moved by physical attraction while women want firm financial support. Ladies get yourself together externally while you are single and it will become a habit you hold onto once married. Men please maintain financial stability. Live your life moderately. The Bible says we should, "Let our moderation be known unto man." LET means you do it. Don't look to follow other people. Expensive toys you don't need don't buy.

Finally, men learn how to be willing to listen more and talk less. Women understand that men find it difficult to emote so when we start talking never interrupt. Get as much out of us as you can because if we sense drama we will shut down. Also, guys remember that unlike women we can't do several things at the same time. A woman can be talking on the phone, cooking, helping the kids with their homework, and a few more things besides those. And she can be doing it all at the same time. She will never miss a beat in any of those tasks. This is a gift almost all women have.

Whereas, if men are on the couch watching television with remote control in hand, we go completely comatose to any conversation someone attempts to start. We simply cannot do it. We have to put the television on mute or turn it off to have a decent conversation. If we don't and she persist it becomes an open door for frustration and annoyance. I honestly hate to mention this but it is the truth and the better men and women know about each other the more harmonious the relationships will actually be.

REALISTIC VIEWS

Now hear this. The only thing a Christian man or woman can honestly expect from one another is what the Bible says. We tend to elevate our expectations higher than what God even expects once we are saved. Whoever God saves is imperfect and he saved you. Many times single Christians never rid themselves of worldly thinking regarding the qualities and character a man or woman should have. When we were not living our life for God we would delete someone out of life at the slightest mistake. But remember all these decisions were made with ungodly knowledge. We must now begin to allow the Bible to govern how we handle all our relationships.

This is the reason the divorce rate in the House of Prayer is higher than the outside world. Now I know percentage wise it's not, but if 66% of 1000 couples in the world divorce and 66% of 100 couples in the church divorce, you still have more couples together in the world than total couples in the church. You see when the percentages of the numbers are in proportion we still lose because we have less people in the church than in the world. More importantly we make a mockery of God and that is number when can never chart.

Expectation requires patience and the understanding that we don't have to compromise and accept just anybody. We ALL are gifts to somebody. Regardless of how difficult the times alone may become do not replace expectation with anxiety. Sometimes the LORD will forsake making a situation better for us but will make us better right in the midst of a situation. In many instances we will focus on what we don't have rather than where we are going. Put a plan together. If you can discern where you are going you will get a better feel for the type of person you need to be expecting. Sometimes we think we know but when don't this is when we should lean on the Word of God.

*Likewise the Spirit also helpeth our infirmities: for we know not what we should pray for as we ought: but the Spirit itself maketh intercession for us with groanings which cannot Be uttered. And he that searcheth the hearts knoweth what is the **Mind of the Spirit**, Because he maketh intercession for the saints according to the will of God. And we know that all things work together for good to them that Love God, to them who are the called according to his purpose.* (Romans 8:26-28)

The people of the world are keenly aware that men and women of God are the best suitors of marriage. Traditionally they have been and it holds true today. I'll tell you something else I firmly believe. The world is hoping we are right. Right about what you ask. Right about everything. Right about salvation, right about relationships, right about the entire counsel of God. When there life of luxury, lust, greed, and pride finally comes to a screeching halt they will come running and kneel at the feet of Jesus and ask what must we do to be saved. That's what I believe. Until then we must press on.

One of the stumbling blocks many singles will incur will be past failures. Some will have to deal with the failures of a parental divorce. This can have a severe effect on their expectations. Fear can easily grip the mind of a Christian if he or she drops their guard. The past doesn't have to affect your present or future. You must decide for yourself if you are going to allow this to happen. The Bible says in 2 Timothy 1:7, "God hath not given us the spirit of fear; but of power, and of love, and of a sound mind."

Fear is a spirit that can be overcome by a Spirit. Not by power, nor by might but by my Spirit is how God intervenes. God has given us a sound mind to use if we so choose. The devil will seek to rob you of your future because of the past if you submit. He will whisper in your ear and make you think you're the only one with that type of past. But he is a liar.

The Bible states in Luke 18:1 that men ought always to pray, and not to faint or lose heart. The first eight verses speak of a widow who continually kept coming and troubling a wicked judge. The ungodly judge had to admit that because of stubbornness he vindicated her. The moral is that when we are expecting from God is never wrong to keep entreating him about what we are seeking. We are urged to always pray. Remember that always praying includes closing our mouths so we may hear from God. It does absolutely no good to always be talking and never listening.

Christian men and women both need to be aware that there will be suitors who will see the Jesus in you and not necessarily you. I must say that for some reason during my backslidden years I was able to procure the company of a lady when I chose to. I mean this in no conceited or prideful manner. I am pretty sure many of you can say the same. For whatever reason there was never a problem getting a date on a Friday night.

However, now that I have turned from life a sin and turned to Jesus I seem to have attracted even more attention from women. I hope somebody is saying "Amen" to this. I refuse to believe I am out here on an island alone on this subject. I have had phone numbers slipped to me before, during, and after church service on many occasions. I have had women blatantly tell me I was their future husband and had other people tell me certain women were "in love" with me. This without a date, phone call, or a kiss. Nothing more than good morning my sister. Now how does a man or woman control something like that? It is simply impossible to even try and understand what is going on in the mind or heart of a person when these types of things happen.

Since I found this so puzzling I went to God in prayer to find answers. Through prayer I was able to ascertain that it was actually the God in me that made me attractive to these women and not necessarily me. God has a way a humbling you. Rather than be disappointed I thanked the LORD and gave him the glory. I'll tell you why. While working on a travel assignment for a consulting company I was informed a young lady was attracted to me.

I dismissed it but wanted to know why the person who was telling me this felt that way. I was told because she now was bringing her Bible to work and studying when she had not been doing that before I showed up. Unfortunately, the person telling me this was a professing

Christian. This is one of the reasons many people in the world are confused about Christians. Rather than joy in this work of God she found a reason to judge the voracity of this women's heart. My question was simply this, if you have been here months before I arrived why didn't she see you and be provoked to open her Bible? Many will say she's trying to get your attention brother so don't be naïve. Well let's say that's true, does it matter. If it took God sending me there to provoke her or anybody else to open their Bibles, and draw closer to God then so be it.

That leads me to believe that's why God sent me there. We can never lose sight for our main purpose in any environment. It is to be a living witness for the LORD Jesus Christ. I realize we all must be cognizant of wolves in sheep's clothing but if I do what I am suppose to do I need not worry about anyone else.

The Bible says we are to put on the full armor of God everyday. This is not to say the person telling me or the person being spoken of were not Christians. There are many carnal Christians in our society today. They are part of the liberal crowd that profess in Jesus as savior but refuse to make him LORD. They profess with their mouths but their hearts are far from God. They believe a change in behavior is unnecessary to be a Christian. They are professing Christians but practicing atheist. The world calls them "Notional Christians" signifying those profess to be Christians but are neither "born again" nor evangelical in behavior. So what should we do? Pray for them and turn it over to God. We who have a relationship rooted in his Word know that God looks on the inside while man looks on the outside. I cannot see what's in and individual's heart.

BACK ON TRACK

These are the type of situations we will be facing but I see as an honor. Anytime I come up against any trying situation I thank God that HE deems me worthy to go through the test. Christians who are weak in faith don't want any heavy trials. They would rather have a watered down gospel preached. They'd prefer church attendance occasionally.

They are fine with paying tithes some weeks or months but not all. They give God little or nothing but expect the world. Your level of expectation from God should be an indication of your giving.

I am by no means talking about money. Though if you are not tithing and supporting your House of Prayer your are robbing God. This thievery is putting a curse on your life and can have an adverse effect on you meeting that future mate. When we rob God he says in the book of Malachi we are cursed. Therefore, if you are part of the people God is talking to pray about it and allow him to get you on track in this particular area of your life. A blessing is waiting to be poured out of the windows of heaven. I would think that a blessing would need to come out of only one window but God says he will open windows just to bless you. Your mate could be behind one of those closed windows. This is why it is so important to study God's Word.

There are things you will never understand and know about God without reading and studying his Word. God has so many ways to get you to the place he wants you to be. He has countless avenues to get the person you should spend you life with to you. I was using the navigational system in the car and it helped me gain a spiritual truth about how God deals with us. When you put your origination address and destination address in the system it computes a route for you to take. It gives you highway, street, and road directions.

As you drive it will even tell you when you need to prepare to turn during your trip. The thing that caught my attention is if you deviate from the route it doesn't just shut down and call you an idiot. It re-computes from where you turned and gives you another route. Now you may lose some time with the new route but you will eventually get to the original destination. Now I could stop there but the system can do better. If you off the original route in excess it could re-compute and give you a new route bypass some highways, some streets, and even some roads and get you to the original destination quicker than the first plan. That is what God can do if you submit to his Holy Ghost power.

Sometimes in life we get off the route God has predestined for us. We all disobey God and find ourselves in a quagmire because we thought we knew what was best for us. No matter how idiotic we may get within ourselves God always remains cool and when we decide to come to ourselves he says do you want me to re-compute? I tell you the more I study, pray, and seek God the dumber I realize I am, but the more I trust him.

When you really begin to fall in love with God there will be no room for arrogance. When I see arrogant Christians I immediately get the feeling they have not fell in love with God. They are saved but are still finding glory in what they are doing. They still find a way to stand up and take credit for something they had no power in their minds or body to do.

That they (us) should seek the LORD, if haply they might feel after him, and find him, Though he be not far from every one of us: For in him we live, and move, and have our Being... (Act 17:27-28)

When you grope for God and find him he becomes your world and nothing else matters. This is important because this is when things come your way. I believe when Christians grope for things it slows down the process immensely. James 4:3 says, "Ye ask, and receive not, because ye ask amiss, that ye may consume it upon your lusts." When we expect things to consume on ourselves and not for the glory of God we don't receive them.

You better remember it does not matter what comes out of our mouths because God knows our hearts. He knows there is wickedness there. So the Word must cleanse our heart. The Word of God replaces us with HIM. I dare you to start expecting God to use you for something other than being a spouse and watch how quickly you find yourself a married man or woman.

I know it doesn't make sense but God's thoughts are not our thoughts and His ways are not our ways. God operates on a different level than we do. That's the bad news. The good new is he wants us on the level. This is why is says in Philippians 2:5, "Let this mind be in you which was also in Christ Jesus." God wants us thinking like him so our expectations and desires line up with his expectations and desires. When we meet new and exciting people we must understand that not every man or woman we meet is the one. You must be able to sense something in the inner most part of your spirit or as the psalmist says, "Deep calling unto deep," is when you will just know. You can't explain it but you just know it. This is not only in relationships, but also in all our decision-making.

Many people make the fatal error of believing just because a man or woman says or makes a nice gesture that person has to be the one. This is totally wrong and you end up coming off as desperate. There will be a certain flow that only can be detected by the inner man when you meet the right person. You may be talking about something so far from romance and a light will suddenly go off. The key is not to rush if this occurs because you cannot move like you move pre-Christ. It is important to take your time and gather yourself before embarking down this road. I am especially talking to men here.

It should be the men making the godly moves if chemistry begins to flow. Always remember the relationship you had up to that point. Never lose sight of what you had before the light went off. If you both mutually agree that taking your friendship to the next level would actually jeopardize the friendship you may want to rethink the whole matter. If either party feels that the friendship would suffer then take a time out. Time outs are not just for children. If more grown men and women took timeouts we would have less marital and relationship problems in and out the church.

KNOW YOUR MOTIVES

Friendships usually end when or suffer when one person ceases to live up to the expectation of the other person. I know people who do not talk to me anymore for the sole reason of I cease to be what they wanted me to be. They had it all planned out about how I would fit in their life and when I didn't comply they departed. I don't worry about it because I know anyone who leaves never intended to stay.

They went out from us, but were not of us; for if they had been of us, they would no Doubt have continued with us: but they went out, that they might be made manifest That they were not all of us. But ye have an unction (anointing) from the Holy One, And ye know all things. (1 John 2:19-20)

God says that those who leave you were never part of the plan he has for you and your life. This is so important because as a single Christians you will be inundated with so many opportunities that you will need the guidance of the Holy One to sort through all the mess.

There will be mess and tons of it. I gave you examples of mess I had to wade through in and outside the church walls. The thing to remember is that if you had a solid friendship with someone in or outside the church, don't be selfish and allow flesh to cloud your judgment. This is another reason abstinence is key to a godly relationship.

Abstinence allows for emotional and compassionate liking. It also allows for two people to develop a caring and understanding attitude for one another. It subsequently fuses a bond between the two people that doesn't hinge upon sex. Sex always changes pre-marital relationships. Paul calls it the joining together or becoming one. There is a tie that occurs when people engage in sexual relations and that is why it should remain in marriage. I'll touch on this later. I promise.

Friendships should be the foundation of all expectant Christian relationships. It does not matter who is involved. Jesus said we were no more servants but friends. If our LORD described his relationship to us in that manner I am positive he expects us to follow his lead with each other. Once you past this stage your expectation come into play more than ever.

I have found that some times I thought I knew what I wanted and had to go back to God. Every man and woman think, act, and react totally different. I have sent flowers to women who thought it was too soon and didn't send to those who thought I was too late. I have been the same nice guy to one and it be considered politeness and another wants to know what time should I pick her up.

I'm putting my business in your hand because I don't know you so if this hits, you can say ouch. I laid down the red carpet and one was ready to roll it back up and the other ready to walk down in a white dress. See I consider myself old school and believe chivalry is not dead. I've sent cards of friendship and had one to say "yes" and another to say "so what." The bottom line is different strokes for different folks.

Let's look at some things women should avoid. Ladies please don't jump to early conclusions about why he did what he did. Some men are real gentlemen and enjoy putting a smile on people's faces. They really don't care who it is or where they are. They get pleasure out of people feeling good. Also, if you are not interested in a young man and you sense he is let him know you are not interested. Contrary to popular belief men can accept rejection. We will not go and jump off a building if you tell us you're not interested. The earlier you tell us the better but please tell us. I think this one can work both ways so men take this advice as well.

In addition, please tell us what you like and dislike. We cannot read minds nor will we try. The more we know about what you expect and want the better we can accommodate thus avoid conflict. And whatever you do not assume you can change anything about our character, personality, or preferences.

If ANY man or woman is expecting God to bless them with someone and they cannot live with that person if they don't change one iota, then you are not ready for a relationship. Do not ever think you can change something about anybody God places in your life. If someone is a Christian and you feel that a change would benefit his or her spiritually, then pray.

You do not have human changing ability but the Holy Spirit does. The Bible says in 1 John 5:14-15, "And this is the confidence that we have in him, that, if we ask any thing according to his will he heareth us. And if we know that he hear us, whatsoever we ask, we know that we have the petitions that we desired of him."

God says when your prayer lines up with my will I will do it. This is something all Christians need to get in there heads and they wouldn't be duped so much. They wouldn't be deceived into sowing this for that and sowing that for this. If it's not lining up with the will of God it's not of God. It can't be put any simpler than that.

Men please listen carefully. Every woman does not have a price tag on her head. Contrary to the ancient myth circulating, all women are not pretentious. Many women today have worked so diligently to procure a life for themselves, that they do not need you to try and buy their love. It will be a plus that you are a man who prides himself in working and taking care of a family. The Bible says if a man would not work he shouldn't eat. It didn't say couldn't work or didn't have a job. It said would not work. Every able-bodied man should and is commanded by God to work.

Do not waste your time trying to convince her to like you any more than she does. I believe in growing and not falling in love. If you fall in love you can fall out. Time will inevitably be the proof of where someone really stands in his or her relationship to you. It is the same with a Christian and his relationship with Jesus and it will be the same with our relationships with each other.

Do not be afraid to share your feeling with the women. This does not make you less than a man. It shows your maturity and gives her confidence that you trust her. Women realize men have a difficult time trusting and anything you do the quench her fears in this area will prove to be a plus for you down the road.

Another important thing you want to do is develop the patience to join her during her shopping expeditions. If you want to know the spending habits of a potential woman don't wait until you say, "I do" because it will be too late. Take some time from watching the game or hanging with the fellows to tag along while she takes a stroll through mall. This is how you find out if she buys out of wants or needs. This is so important because money is the number one cause of friction between married couples.

Either she spends too much or he spends too much. He is parsimonious or she takes frugality to the limit. She shops too much or he spends to big. He needs to make more she needs to budget better. It helps to understand why God says, "The love of money is the root of all evil." Now that love doesn't necessarily mean someone who just love to make and have a bunch for selfish spending. The aforementioned examples fall into this love. When we forget that God blesses us with money and all us are to be faithful stewards over that money we allow all kinds of problems to occur, thus the root of evil.

CAN YOU HANDLE IT

Guys please don't expect God to bless you with a smart, educated, and independent woman then become jealous and intimidated by those very qualities. In the book of Judges God shows gives us a panoramic view of a strong, mighty, God-fearing woman and a husband who remained confident in himself despite her stature. Judges 4:4 says, "And Deborah, a prophetess the wife of Lapidoth, she judged Israel at that time." See when God needs to get something done the best man for the job might just have to be a woman. The absence of an anointed man of God will never stop God from doing what he's going to do.

The Bible says that Deborah judged Israel at that time. She was married yet she judged Israel. She was a prophetess yet she judged Israel. She was a woman yet she judged Israel. Here me when I say that all of that is simply awe inspiring. But the most awe-inspiring thing about her judging Israel was her husband felt intimidated by her position. She didn't have to fight with him about what God had done in her life. She didn't have to give an account to why God used her and didn't perhaps use him.

She was free from stress to do God's will because of the maturity of Lapidoth. He took pride in her wisdom and decision making ability. And in the midst of it all he never lost his position in the house. Because Deborah was a godly woman I know for sure she was quite the wife at home. There are lessons for both sides here.

My brother's can you stand to be blessed with Deborah type women. Three raised me so I am seeking such. Ladies can you be a juggernaut in the workplace and be used mightily by God outside the home and come back to the home and be submissive according to scripture? There so much in that one scripture regarding Deborah if I was the get in it I could write an entire chapter about strong women and the men in their lives. Since I can let's go to the next chapter.

SIX
What Did God Say?

And the LORD God said, It is not good
That the man should be alone; I will
Make him a helpmeet for him. (Genesis 2:18)

The reason it is so important I discuss this is because of the role society has forced women to play. Because of the lack of solid male leadership in homes women have been called on to increase their roles in the family. And since families have become non-traditional (that is having only one parent) women have found their responsibilities increased immeasurably. I am aware there are men who are single parents and by no means attempt to diminish their role but more often than not this scenario is female dominated.

Therefore, women are being raised with the mind set that a man is not needed. They are raised with the mentality that they don't need a man be successful in society. Man-less mothers who have no example to give them as to why a two parent house if what God desires are raising them. The conversation usually contains the proverbial "if I could raise you by myself without a man you don't need one either." But I ask, "What does God say."

The list of accomplishments will flow freely from the mother's lips.

I went to college. I got my degree. I got a job with a Fortune 500 company. I moved up the corporate ladder. When I birthed you and he left I didn't miss a beat seeing you were well taken care of.

And with all that being said I ask, "What does God say." There will be the list of accomplishments by the child whether it is a boy or girl. You did this and you did that and you were the head of your class with this and you led the state in that. And once again I will ask, "What does God say."

Well God felt man should not be alone and upon this belief decided to do something about it. What he did was create woman. Mind you I said woman and not women. He took a rib not ribs from Adam body. Why would God do this for man? Well here in lies the problem. We assume God did it for man because he said man should not be alone. But let us take a look back in a previous chapter. Genesis 1:26 says, "…God said, Let us make man in our image, after our likeness: and let them have dominion over the fish of the sea, and over the fowl of the air, and over the cattle, and over all the earth, and over every creeping thing that creepeth upon the earth." God said let's create man and let them have dominion.

Couple with this verse with verse twenty-eight that says, "God blessed them, and God said unto them, Be fruitful, and multiply, and replenish the earth, and subdue it." God created men and women so he could have godly seed reproduced on earth. Malachi 2:15-16 says, "And did not he make one? Yet had the residue of the spirit. And wherefore one? That he might seek a godly seed (remnant). Therefore take heed to your spirit, and let none deal treacherously against the wife of his youth. For the LORD, the God of Israel, saith that he hateth putting away (divorce)."

God so desires to have this world replenished with godly people living holy lives. This was he sought when he first created Adam. But with the same freedom Adam had we use that freedom to live completely opposite of what God says. God wants godly men and women to marry and have children. Raise them up in a godly fashion and then they meet other godly people and they have children and so forth and so on. This is why single parenting is totally against what God wants. Listen I am a product of a single parent home but could it be that this is why I am still single? I have to use myself as an example because if I talk about others so of you may get upset. So I'll use myself as much as possible. There may be instances where I just can't help myself so charge it to my hear and not my heart. Amen.

When a man and woman of God marry and have children and in turn raise those very children according to what the Bible says I can't help but believe that regardless of what happens in that child's life eventually it will end at the foot of God. That being said I feel it necessary to mention that if a child is raised in a home with just one godly parent the same outcome is plausible.

I am aware that a many preacher kids have grown up and turned out to be nothing more than the devil. I know that but this is where freedom of choice comes in. But if they have a foundation rooted in the Word of God the chances for them are much higher than someone raised outside a godly family. The chances I am talking about have nothing to do with worldly achievement. Remember the wise things of the world are foolishness to God.

If you live long enough you will know that there will be blessings and calamity in life. So we can never look at the world's version of success once become a Christian. The world would think a multi-millionaire who doesn't care one bit about Jesus is in better position than a homeless saint. Thank God the world will not be the final judge. God says in Psalms 14:1, "The fool hath said in his heart, There is no God."

God considers any man who says there is no God to be a fool. He did not mention any specific man when he said this only that if he did not believe he was a fool. See God thinks it utterly ridiculous to have been created by him and yet not believe in him. I am not going to get to deep into what people think, but for all people who do believe that we have created by God why would you not submit to that God? Why wouldn't you seek that God to answer the questions life presents? Why wouldn't someone take full advantage of having the answers to an exam and it not be considered cheating?

Genesis 1:1 says, "In the beginning God created the heaven and the earth." Therefore, if there are any questions we have regarding any subject in life, where do you think we should go for answers? How about the Word of God that is the Bible. That is a rhetorical question and I will answer it for you. God has created the heaven and the earth. He created us to live on the earth and desires we not be alone. Then why are so many of us alone?

RISE OF WOMEN

Let's take a gander into this complex question. Women in this country more than ever have been blessed by God to be elevated in all areas of society. Having once been outcast and downtrodden under the foot of domineering men they are now in the dubious position of leading. In many cases they have surpassed men and created a power struggle, which has bled into the area of romance.

I don't think and this is just my opinion that men of any substance lay awake at night sleepless because women are growing in stature the every work industry imaginable. I don't think these types of men are. There are insecure and immature men who may lose sleep but I wouldn't think the aforementioned men do. But you know I have been wrong in my life before and I could actually be wrong again. My ears are actually itching and burning because I can hear some ladies saying, "you don't know some of the men I work with." So I will just assume and hope this assumption doesn't cause too much friction. I know for a fact that I don't lose sleep regarding the success of woman and if you are a Christian man and you can't stand to see successful women you should be ashamed.

By the same token if you are a single Christian and you feel this way you could be single for a long time. I myself find it quite attractive that a woman has used the talents and gifts God gave her to do something for him. Notice I said does something for him.

Back to my original thought regarding why so many of us are single. In the previous chapter I gave an example of a powerful woman of God named Deborah and her husband Labidoth. Let's revisit their marriage. Deborah was called and used by God during a time when there was no king in Israel. This is a period in the Bible God used Judges to do just that. This was one of the most chaotic times in human history. Judges 21:25 says, "In those days there was no king in Israel: every man did that which was right in his own eyes." Now take that and juxtapose it with Proverbs 14:12 which says, "There is a way which seemeth right unto a man; but the end thereof are the ways of death" and you understand why there was such chaos.

Nevertheless, despite the chaotic state Israel was in, God saw fit that a woman would be hold this most noted position. The fact God inserted this woman in this position clearly shows God will not allow any plan he has to be negated because men refuse to rise to the occasion. I applaud the work of Deborah and how God so wonderfully used her. I applaud every Christian woman who God is using today. I feel this is what makes our God so awesome. To know he can get the job done regardless of gender or race. Hallelujah.

MEN IN CHARGE

I now want to focus on Lapidoth who was the husband of Deborah. We don't read much about him except that he was her husband. But when I think about the lack of scripture regarding Lapidoth I am reminded of another man who name is mentioned only minimum in scripture. That man's name is Joseph. I am not talking about Jacob's son Joseph but the husband of the Mary. Yes, Mary the mother of our LORD and Savior Jesus Christ. The last thing I recall about Joseph is something quite noteworthy it occurs in Luke 2:51 and describes what happened once Jesus was located by Joseph and Mary.

This scripture says Jesus went down with them to Nazareth from Jerusalem and was subject unto them. There is so much you can get out of one scripture. What I get out of the scripture that tells me about Lapidoth and this scripture about Joseph is powerful. These two scriptures tell me that God doesn't just give special people to anybody.

The mother of Jesus was hand picked by God and rightfully so but do you think God did not take into account who she was betrothed to. When the Holy Ghost came upon Mary and she conceived could you imagine what a lesser man than Joseph would have done?

We understand from reading that Joseph was called a just and upright man. Therefore, because he did not want to make her a public spectacle he sought to divorce her secretly. Although they were not married to be betrothed was just a one-year prelude to the eventual nuptial. But as he thought about what he would do the angel of the LORD appeared and explained everything to him.

Now an immature and insecure man today wouldn't want to hear anything from an angel or Mary. She is engaged to be married and he knows he is waiting for their honeymoon before becoming intimate and she approaches him a few nights before the wedding with some big news. Can you imagine a woman approaching a man today with the phrase a man never likes to hear, honey we need to talk. I know the fellows know what I mean. In the history of my life I cannot ever remember anything good being said after that particular phrase. Even when it's not bad news it's bad news. If the man doesn't end up hot under the collar he ends up speechless. Either way it's never good.

But you see God knew Joseph was the right man for Mary so don't you believe it was not divine intervention that put them together. Think for a moment my sisters on a time when you did utter the above phrase and some guy went completely off on you. And think again when you uttered that phrase and a brother was cool as a cucumber. I said it is never good to hear that phrase but we all don't take it the same way. More often than not what is said after the phrase will be the kicker regarding our ultimate reaction.

Nevertheless, God knew Joseph and Lapidoth were the perfect compliments for the women who would mightily use. Thus, you ladies who are enjoying wonderful worldly success you must seek God more than ever to know if the guy who appears as your knight in shining armor is going to have the intestinal fortitude to handle any success you may have or end up acquiring. As sanctified as that man may feel he is he still has feelings and wants to feel like you have need of him.

Remember it was God who called Eve a helpmeet. A helpmeet is someone who is comparable to another. She was supposed to be one who would help supply that which Adam could not supply for himself.

When needed Adam was to summon her help and know she was ready, willing, and able to comply. As she fulfilled the help part she would also fulfill the meet portion by complementing him as his equal.

One of the problems we have is that some men and women don't understand that the woman was always suppose to be equal to man and not on the level of the other earthly creatures. Adam was to have dominion over everything except Eve. I know am treading in deep water but since I am out here I might as well keep going.

There are Christian or professing Christian men who happen to know exactly one scripture in the bible other than John 3:16. They probably can't tell you where it is and I'm not going to tell them now, but it says a woman is suppose to be submissive to her husband. I must admit they actually have it right. They just don't have it completely right. The scripture says, "Wives, submit yourselves unto your own husbands, as unto the LORD." This means that wives are suppose to submit to their husbands in the same manner that they would submit to Christ. However, when you guys find this scripture look directly at the scripture before it. That scripture says, "Submitting yourselves one to another in the fear of God."

This is key because she is submitting just as you are submitting. This means she's not submitting to an emotional, physical, or psychological abuser. She is submitting to someone who has submitted himself to God. I know many preachers who teach that regardless of his behavior women should still submit. I say the devil is a liar. If a man is abusive and dangerous you leave him right where he is and if you must submit then do it from your momma's house.

You are not a punching bag and you are not his child. If he doesn't have the decency and understanding to know his dominion after the animals and before you point him to the first book in the Bible. I didn't mean to go off on tangent, but I simply detest men who are so cowardly they must find a woman to take their frustrations out. Women have arguably made the greatest leap of any group of people in society. If you read scripture they were viewed sometimes on the level of animals. This is what makes their ascension so great. They were never meant to be at that level yet that is where men put them. So they found themselves debased, ostracized, scorned, and mistreated. Here women are made to be a helper equal to men but denigrated to the point of humiliation.

But God in his wisdom gave them intellect and knowledge which would catapult them right back into the upper echelon of society's consciousness. This is why some Christian and non-Christian men have developed a complex with independent women. They read the Bible, read history books, and hear stories of the past and can't understand how women were able to crawl from under all of the muck and mire men buried them with and stand up and say, "We're still here." And not only back, but also back with a vengeance.

This is resurgence by women has ultimately proved to be more detrimental for the perpetrator than for the women who were initially wronged. Men now find themselves competing in every field of life with the very people they sought to demoralize. This has now demoralized the men and caused a reversal of fortune never before witnessed. This shift is more profound than the improvements made by blacks and other minorities.

So this is what men have to go up against. Women pass on the experience of different trials and tribulations that men have taken them through and each generation vows to never allow a man to hold her down. Therefore, when a man comes with the proposition of marriage it is viewed as a camouflaged attempt to stunt her growth as a woman. I am just explaining this from a male point of view. I could be wrong concerning some of these observations but I know I am not wrong about them all. I know because I have experienced it first hand.

I have been conversing with a lady and said something that touched a sore spot and an adverse reaction soon followed. Something along the lines of "my last boyfriend use to do that and I'll never go through that again." Does that sound familiar to anyone? She has made her mind up that she will never go through whatever it is again. I could have been making an off-the-cuff statement and I end up getting the past boyfriend comparison. This has happened countless times I must say. So I have some experience in these matters.

Women now more than ever feel there will be a host of suitors just waiting to sweep them off their feet. I say be careful ladies because time is not on any of our sides. Job 14:1-2 says, "Man that is born of a woman is of few days, and full of trouble. He cometh forth like a flower and is cast down or fades away." It is dangerous to think like the heathens and feel you have all the time in the world to make a connection. If you truly believe in a soul mate then you know that it is a person tailor-made for you and only you. Therefore, when he comes you better be spiritually grounded that you know this is who you have been waiting for.

TEAMWORK IS KEY

It really saddens me when I read articles or hear stories about so-called professional women thumbing their noses at blue collar working men. This annoys me period but even more when I hear Christian women speaking in this way. How dare a women God has blessed to do whatever she is doing think she should be with a man for his social or economic status. I cannot think of anything sadder about a woman other than her not being saved. To reject someone because of their occupation or career choice is one of the shallowest things a woman can ever do. It signifies that she is concerned with what other people think. That to me is very interesting because I'm thinking if you were as concerned with what God thinks you would have less time to focus on people.

Also, at the end of the day what does it really matter? When both of you arrive home from a hard day at your respective jobs who outside your home really cares that he is pulling off a dirty uniform and you are taking off a two-piece suit. If you care what your single girlfriend at work says then you may need to find new girlfriends. But please don't get rid of the man because the deceit in the human heart tells me your girlfriend will be first in line to snatch him up.

Ladies if you have a man and he makes less money, or works blue collar and you happen to make more money and work white collar when, when the money goes into the account does it really matter? Now I am not talking about folks living together outside marriage because I don't believe in that. I have done it before and I wouldn't do it again. The only reason needed to give why I wouldn't is if she is good enough to move in with she is good enough to marry. That is my take on that and if you are a Christian and God hasn't opened your spiritual eyes to see it this way pray and ask him to and I know he will.

One reason the pretentious attitude that this type of woman displays is immature is that all money is not quality money. I'll explain. When the National Basketball Association locked their players out and there was not basketball fans found out something that they might not have known. Just because a person makes five million dollars a year that doesn't mean he is wealthy. He may be rich so don't get me wrong but wealth and rich are not the same thing. I heard a comedian say what I am about to say but I knew this from reading finance books. The player playing the game is rich but the owner writing and signing the checks is wealthy.

There were players who owned million dollar homes, several cars, jewelry, and closets full of clothes, yet did not have a five figures in the bank. They were living paycheck to paycheck just like some people who have five figure salaries. Just because a person has a large salary, that is in no way an indication of their wealth. Wealthy CEOs are as inconspicuous as they come yet the money they earn sometimes doubles and triples that of the wealthiest athlete.

There are men who are so rooted and grounded in the Word of God could care less about what the world thinks of them. Thus, they live a moderated lifestyle and believe in putting money back into God's hand for the proclaiming of the gospel. Now you think a man who lives is life in this fashion is not wealthy because his salary is 50k per year. I know people who live just like this and have well over six and sometimes seven figures in accounts. They don't need the latest name brand clothing. One car is enough for them to own at one time. They take care of their clothes and only purchase when needed and bridle their wants.

These are the things godly Christians should do. So here you have a man who loves God and lives as I have just described. He leaves home for work everyday in hard hat and boots. The woman leaves home in the latest style of dress in her expensive automobile with her ungodly expensive purse. She drives the expensive car to work and parks. She gets out of the expensive car wearing her expensive clothes and carrying her expensive purse. She enters her office wearing her expensive clothes and puts down her expensive purse while her expensive car waits to be driven eight hours later. She proceeds to sit at her desk and work on he computer all day excluding lunch. She may see a client or she may not. The day ends at five and she reverses what she did earlier that morning.

Somebody please write me and explain to me what does it matter? She just as well went to work in a jump suit driving a truck. This is pride. We are supposed to possess things and things not possess us. Any woman who has issues with a blue-collar man who makes less money is an empty individual. I must warn you about something. Every guy who is considered blue collar doesn't necessarily make less money than your white-collar counterparts. Some of the same men you drive past, who are working on road construction earn more than some of the same men working in your office

Also, if you are a woman who has those women who must possess all of the trappings of the rich and famous you honestly need to increase you walk with God. We are stewards over God's money. Yes, God's money. Jesus told us to occupy and do business until he returns. Remember the parable about the talents? Well remember the owner did return. He tends to focus on the fact he took the one talent from the sluggard but remember he did return to find out what they had done.

It is God who promotes and not man. It is God who blesses us with jobs. I know you think it was your degree or your intellect but whom do you think gave you the intellect to get the degree? Who do you think gave you those stunning good looks? If God removed his glory from your life right now you wouldn't know what you were reading. When you view life from God's perspective you will never find any reason to be prideful about anything.

Leave that to the people who don't know Jesus. We know better thus let's rid ourselves of that carnal thinking. If a man were living for God and desires to be with you, it would behoove you to give him a fair shake. As I will explain the final chapter the harvest may be plenty for souls needing to be saved but the pickings are getting mighty slim for potential mates.

KNOW YOUR ROLE

God has gotten this crazy idea that men should be the head of house regardless of what the woman says. I don't know where God could have come up with this but for some reason he has. And since I have found that arguing with God gets you nowhere and gets you there fast I will just have to go with this one, albeit kicking and screaming. God views man as the stronger vessel. That means he views women as the weaker vessel. Because of this he doesn't leave the women without his protection

He says in 1 Peter 3:7, "…ye husbands, dwell with them according to knowledge, giving honor unto the wife, as unto the weaker vessel, and as heirs together of the grace of life; that your prayers be not hindered.

In the prior verse God gave us a perfect example of woman to man submission by telling us how Sarah obeyed Abraham by calling him lord. He even says you are daughters of Sarah and should do as well. I know what you ladies are thinking. Abraham wasn't always the sharpest knife in the bunch but he was God's man and that is all that matters. When God gives you a man believe me he will not be perfect. But he will be your man and you should dwell with him Sarah dwelt with Abraham. I want the men to notice what God says in that seventh verse because it some strong talk in there.

First of all he let's us know he is speaking directly to the husbands. This is interesting because he was just talking about Sarah. See God doesn't waste time or words when it comes to the family. He finishes talking about how women should emulate Sarah and jumps right on the men. Ye husbands, dwell. Dwell means to take up residence. It doesn't mean to hang out or visit occasionally or let the home be a place to change clothes. Men you should desire a wife that you can do anything with. You shouldn't want a wife who you can do some things with.

I know I want a wife who is as comfortable watching the ball game as she is watching romance movies. And I understand she should expect the same thing. So dwell is to be grounded by the root. The same way the Holy Spirit dwells or tabernacles with us we should do the same with our wives. Second, he says husbands dwelling should be according to knowledge. What knowledge is God talking about? He is talking about understanding that she is your wife and deserves honor. It is tied to the next stanza that says giving honor unto the wife. This is the knowledge you should use when dwelling.

Of course this comes from a relationship with the Bible and paying attention to the woman herself. Paying attention to her when she expresses concerns, desires, dislikes, and tendencies. This can also include remembering your anniversary, her birthday, and other special days. These things may mean absolutely nothing to some men but they mean the world to women and to dwell according to knowledge is to let things that are important to her become important to you. If you honor her in public she is sure to show appreciation and reward you in private. I'll give you guys that one for free. You have to pay for the rest.

Third, he says understand that she is the weaker vessel. You know the more I study the Word of God the more I realize that sin has put us in a terrible state. One wouldn't think some of the things God says he would have to say, but he does. And God doesn't waste words so when he makes a statement it must be important. Men please understand that women are the weaker vessel.

You just can't handle women any kind of way. I am not just talking physical but also any manner. She should be spoken to in a certain manner. There are ways in which you can get your point across without demeaning her. Husbands should never chide their wives in public and wives never do that to your husband. Be of one mind having compassion one to another is what God commands.

Fourth, he says to be heirs together of the grace of life. What good does it do for a couple to marry and then not enjoy the fruit that comes from being husband and wife? There are many benefits to being married and all you need to do is re-read this book to know that. Single Christians who desire to please God are in a battle trying to stay chaste. Unfortunately, I know of many Christians who have married and are not enjoying the spouse they so richly desired.

If you are married and not happy with the relationship then change it. If you sow change you will reap change. Don't waste your life in a situation that doesn't have to be the way it is. Do something about your situation if you don't like it. This is for any area not just relationship wise.

Finally, and most important God says to do all those things will prevent him from shutting his ears to your request. Husbands you do not want God to ever close his ears to your prayers. The Old Testament tells of a godly king named Hezekiah and his request for extended life.

Hezekiah was told to get his house in order because he was going home to be with the LORD. One would think when the prophet Isaiah delivered this news he would be elated but instead he cried and prayed for extended life. God granted him fifteen more years to his life at Hezekiah request.

What God did after granting him the fifteen years is something no man should ever want God to do. 2 Chronicles 32:31 says, "…God left him, to try (test) him, that he might know all that was in his heart." My brothers and sisters pray to God he never leaves you as he did Hezekiah. Pray he never closes his ears to your prayers. Some may be asking why would God need to test Hezekiah's heart? Some of you may be saying to yourself I thought God knew everything. You are one hundred percent correct.

When you read a scripture such as this please understand that God tested Hezekiah to show Hezekiah his own heart. Remember that Hezekiah had prayed and cried to God about how much he loved and adore God. Yet, when this life was spared he displayed an arrogance he never knew was in his heart.

God knows all about you my friends but you don't know about yourself. This is why I have learned not to say what I won't never drink, smoke, or do. Because I know if God ever removes his glory from my life the list of things I am open to doing is endless. Now I know none of the holy rollers reading this book would never admit to something like that but just keep waking up everyday and you might get the test of your life. Pride is just as rampant in the House of God as it is anywhere else. I'll prove it to you through scripture.

PRIDE DIVIDES

In the Gospel of St. Luke chapter number eighteen our LORD and Savior Jesus Christ tell us a parable regarding a Pharisee and publican. The Pharisee represents the Sunday morning church attendee. He/she believes in keeping all the law of God. Always shows up in the best of their religious regalia. Long dresses, big hats, three piece suits, and bible in hand. The publican represents the sinner coming to God with a contrite heart.

Let's begin with verse number nine of Luke 18. The Bible says, "And he spake this parable unto certain which trusted in themselves that they were righteous, and despised others. Already we see Jesus is about to go off just by the audience of pious and self-righteous he is addressing. Verse ten says two men went up into the temple to pray, the one a Pharisee, and the other a publican or tax collector. Now don't miss this in verse eleven. Eleven says The Pharisee stood and prayed thus with himself, God I thank thee, that I am not as other men are, extortioners, unjust, adulterers, or even as this publican (tax collector). It gets better in verse twelve as he continues by saying I fast twice in the week, and I give tithes of all I possess.

Did you read that? Jesus has been crucified, buried, and risen two thousand years later you tell me you don't hear that from church folk today. From the pulpit to the door the House of God reeks with this kind of pride and arrogance. What is said is that Jesus said when he stood and prayed he didn't even realize he was praying to himself because God wasn't even listening. God had completely shut his ears to this self-righteous hypocrite. He boasted of all his works and went down his list of things he didn't do and God wasn't even listening.

Let's continue because this is good. Verse thirteen says the publican (tax collector) standing afar off, would not lift up so much as his eyes unto heaven, but smote (beat) upon his breast, saying, God be merciful to me a sinner. What was the conclusion in the manner? Let's see what Jesus had to say about this church attendee and this sinner.

In verse number fourteen Jesus says I tell you, this man went down to his house justified rather than the other: for every one that exalteth himself shall be abased; and he that humbleth himself shall be exalted.

Was that not an interesting and comparable to the perfunctory and pious folk we come across weekly in the House of God. And it is not just pew sitters. It is pastors, deacons, ministers, elders, choir members, ushers, and greeters. This is why it makes absolutely no sense to judge anyone externally. God looked directly into the heart of both of these men and immediately opened the heavens for the man church folk would have deemed the least. God says the first shall be last and the last shall be first. Of course the world thinks completely opposite but remember we are not of the world.

I told the story of the Pharisee and the publican for one simple reason. Christian singles must always be aware of pride and arrogance. I honestly feel this is an area that keeps many of us from having all of the earthly blessings the Father would have us to have. God has said that man (which includes both sexes) should not be alone. But how many times have you heard a man or woman of God say, "I don't need a husband" or "I don't need a wife." You may not feel you need one but I ask what does God say?

The thing we must understand is there are blessings in which we as singles will never achieve without a mate. God will keep his promises and supply all of our needs but what about some of the wants we desire. Some of those wants could be tied into our mate. I am sure you have heard the expression "Soul Tie." Well let's look at that from a different perspective. Rather than view this from a viewpoint of an internal or spiritual connection, let's take a look at how this might affect things we desire in life.

Some of us may have desire to want a house but God wants us to have a home. A house is physical structure in which we live. We work and save to put ourselves in the best position possible just to purchase a house. But during the entire process God is thinking you really wouldn't have to work that hard if you would accept my help.

Many would assume God's help comes only through money or a yes on the loan application. But God wants more for you. You see a snapshot of you in the house but God sees a home. He sees you and your spouse living together in the house creating a family. A home in an ungodly neighborhood that will stand as a witness to him. He sees the family rising on Sunday mornings and going to church while others rise to go golf. He sees your family being a pillar of unselfishness in the community while others remain aloof and selfish. Remember God wants us to represent him hear on earth. He wants us to be baby Jesus' so to speak. A replica of his son Jesus Christ.

There are many people living in exclusive communities that God desires to send someone into. He seeks a family to plant in an area that may not have been able to be planted in any other human way. Some of us want a house and it seems no matter what we do it just doesn't want to come to fruition. I know there are many who will say "I don't need anyone to buy my own house" and this is the pride I am talking about. This is the exact type of talk God truly detest.

This is why the world is infested with hate and discontent. Christians who still attach the word "my" to everything they possess. Can you imagine the impact Christians could have in society if our stuff becomes God's stuff? That is not a rhetorical question. I want you to ask yourself this most important question and then wait for an answer.

If we continue to do view the things we have belonging to us, how can God ever use it? If it's your car then God will never be able to put some sinner in it. If it's your house God will never be able to have a Bible study in it. If the clothes you wear belong to you then someone needy will never get clothed. This is serious business folks and we need to realize God doesn't like this attitude.

These six things doth the LORD hate; yea, seven are an abomination unto him: A proud look, a lying tongue, and hands that shed innocent blood, A heart that Deviseth wicked imaginations, feet that be swift in running to mischief, A false Witness that speaketh lies, and he that soweth discord among brethren. (Proverbs 6:16-19)

I beseech you my brethren if you find yourselves treading on any one of these you should immediately seek God's face to deliver you. When scripture tells us that God Almighty hates something it was behoove us to make sure that in which he hates his deleted from our lives. Pride is what caused Satan's fall from heaven.

He was an anointed cherub tasked with leading praise and worship in heaven. He allowed himself to become haughty in his own sight and found himself permanently separated from God. In addition, he took a third of the angels with him. It is one thing to be disobedient to God but please don't take innocent people with you. This only adds to the enmity that will be between you and God.

When we don't check ourselves in these areas we become our worst enemy. Someone has said that enemy is "in of me." That flesh man which doesn't want to do things God's way. God told Satan he was perfect in all his ways from the day he was created but then iniquity was found in himself. If you recall my example regarding Hezekiah you see a comparison right here with Satan.

As Christians we may think we've got our ducks in a row. People may applaud us and tell us how wonderful we are. Hear me when I tell you this and never forget it. When you hear these things being said about you don't believe it.

The more people praise you the more you better start praising God. The more people lift you up the more you better fall on your face and lift up the name of Jesus. When Moses would finish talking to God at Mount Sinai he would return to speak to the children of Israel. When he came down the glory of God would be shining upon his face.

The people were fascinated when they gazed upon the man of God. Now wouldn't it have been ignorant of Moses to allow himself to be puffed up. The glory they were witnessing had absolutely nothing to do with Moses.

When Jesus saddled the donkey and road into Jerusalem something magnificent occurred. The people spread garment in the way, cut down branches from trees, and spread them in the road. Others even cried out Hosanna that means please save. Now think for a moment about how asinine it would have been for the ass to think all of that was for him.

Believe me when I tell you there is Christians blessed by God who truly believe it is all about them. As single Christians we have a great work available if we will submit the indwelling power of the Holy Spirit. It is simply no limit to a Christian who does the work of God without being concerned about getting any credit. This is an attitude God enjoys rewarding here on earth. God says in Mark 10:29-30, "...no man that hath left house, or brother, or sisters, or father, or mother, or wife, or children, or lands, for my sake, and the gospels. But he shall receive a hundredfold now in this time, houses, and brothers, and sisters, and mothers, and children, and lands, with persecutions; and in the world to come eternal life."

There is your scripture proof to back up what I said concerning things we possess. When we begin to see all possessions belonging to God he can really use us. The thing is you will never consider the house, car, land, or anything else as God's property until you consider yourself as God's property. The first thing he wants is you. Once he gets you completely everything else should fall in line. Notice I said should because the more I live the more I understand what God meant by presenting us a living sacrifice. I know living sacrifices tend to get up or crawl off the altar. We are walking the spiritual walk and living for God one moment and doing our own carnal thing the next. Holiness unto God requires commitment.

When we relinquish the rights to our lives to God he can truly do a marvelous work even we will be proud of. I look back on my life and I thank God as if I am his parent. I thank him and praise him as if to say look at what you did with the mess I made. I know I didn't clean up my past. It had to be the handiwork of Almighty God. Because of his mercy he allowed me lend minor support but that is it. He seeks an opportunity to do the same in our single life as Christians.

BE A LEADER

I am not an old man but I do remember a time when the man received gratification and self worth from going out and working for his family. I remember when women were happy and satisfied with what they were doing as homemakers. There was godly foundation rooted in men and women that provoked them to want a godly home. A godly home meant the man leaving home daily, working, and bringing home the bacon. It saw the woman taking care of the children and the home. This seems to be an atypical rather than the norm today. Why?

I feel one reason is the effect men and women have allowed the corporate America society to have on the home. Corporate America is not family oriented. It is dollar oriented. Companies today will set up everything you need right on their grounds. If you need daycare its on the grounds. If you need a food and recreation its on the grounds. If you need marital advice its on the grounds. They try to do any and everything to prevent you from needing to spend any unnecessary time at home. This is only one of the reasons I feel the godly home structure has been replaced.

You take this and add competition between the man and woman for jobs and you have a recipe for gender segregation. The women are on one side bickering and complaining about an area they should be willing to relinquish to the man. The men are now devising ways to circumvent any growth by the career minded women. This causes more conflict than the naked eye can see. A deep-rooted breach is created that can only be restored by the hand of Almighty God. Many times man creates a problem that cannot be mended by the one who created it. This is why church leaders and churches should never seek to look like corporate America. The House of God should always seek to be family oriented because that is what we are. We are called the Household of Faith. We are a Spiritual House with Jesus as chief cornerstone. A business attitude is not the attitude to have when dealing with people.

This is how many Christians view relationships and that is wrong. I have heard Christians say that marriage is a business. Where is that in the Bible? One day the church is going to become the bride of Christ. Do you really feel our God considers this a business decision? We have allowed our minds to become so polluted with the mess of the world it's a wonder any singles even want to get married.

God says man should not be alone. What are we going to do with that statement? If there are Christians who have a desire to adhere to the words of God there are some things you must know. Marriage takes a total commitment from two parties. Not one but two participants willing to work together for God. This institution created by God requires communication, compromise, sharing, and sacrifice. Not you must understand that because of our inherited nature these things are opposite of who are what you desire.

People by nature are greedy, arrogant, selfish, and controlling. From the time we come out the womb until conversion we have no desire to do any good in the sight of God. This is why in the gospel of St. John and chapter number three Jesus tells the Pharisee Nicodemus that all men must be "born again." This spiritual quickening or life giving birth allows us to exhibit the qualities which marriage requires. This is also the reason God says Christians should not be unequally yoked together with non-believers. If you are a "born again" Christian and you are dating a non-Christian can you see why there will be conflict.

Both of you are not even on the same plain from a spiritual standpoint. There will be things you should be doing that make absolutely no sense to the non-Christian person. Your willingness to get up on Sunday mornings and go to the House of God may seem like a waste of time to a non-Christian. The desire to sing in a choir, usher, or serve anywhere in the church could be viewed as futile and worthless. Therefore, we must take time to probe one another through conversation to gauge the intentions of every potential mate. There will be people who like something about you who will send their representative out on a date and leave their true person at home. You meet a complete imposter and not the real individual.

This is why we must consistently retain a prayerful attitude so we can always be in a position to discern what God wants from us. Think about this for a moment if you will. One day Jesus hears his friend Lazarus is sick and then he hears he has died. Jesus goes down to Bethany to perform one of his most popular miracles. I want you to take some time and read the entire eleventh chapter of the gospel of St. John and review what I am about to say.

Our LORD and Savior Jesus Christ travels from the east side of Jordan to a village on the Mount of Olives on the road from Jerusalem to Jericho. He has his disciples with him and journeys there with the intention to do one thing. Jesus is going to raise a man who has been dead for four days. Jesus converses with the sisters of the deceased and request to be led to the tomb. I am going somewhere so bare with me. Jesus comes to the tomb groaning within himself. Now think for a moment about the enormous miracle our Savior is about to pull off.

One would think he would have a long and drawn out prayer to the Father but what do we read. John 11:41-42 says, "…Father, I thank thee that thou hast heard me. And I knew that thou hearest me always: but because of the people which stand by I said it, that they may believe that thou hast sent me." He tells Lazarus to come forth and commands the people to loose him, and let him go. What gets lost in this story is the prayer of Jesus.

What we can learn from this is that because of the many hours Jesus spent in prayer with the Father he needed only thirty seconds of prayer to raise a man dead for four days. This is so powerful because we have the third person of the triune God in the person of the Holy Spirit indwelling in us. What I am saying through this story is when we spend time with God he allows us the ability to immediately discern whether a man or woman who is in our midst is for us or not. We don't need to run back to our prayer closet and spend days holed up seeking an answer regarding some potential mate. God can speak to you right there while you are sharing lunch or while having phone conversation. We tend to get real deep and religious when we shouldn't. It would be foolish to think that God desires for man not be alone then not help connect us with someone who won't leave us ALONE. That is not the God we serve my friends. God wants to be involved in the process if we would only let him. Remember God made the Adam and Eve holy and happy. They were not in want or need for anything.

MAKE A DECISION

Some of you are dating someone right now who God has connected you to and your refuse to do the right thing. You are waiting for the perfect time. There is no perfect time. There will never be a perfect time to get married. Some are waiting for the perfect job, promotion, house, and God knows what else. If you are in this group you are playing with fire. Because what you are doing is giving the enemy an opportunity to destroy what God has put together.

Adam and Eve didn't had it all and only needed to enjoy life, yet Satan comes in and convinces them that God is holding out. You can get more and be more. You can be like god and know what's best for you. This is what you open yourself up to when you don't realize you have what you always wanted.

On the other hand, some of you are with someone God has told you to leave. There is no compatibility whatsoever. You don't see eye to on anything. Your relationship is so far from being credible of marriage it is a pure shame. But rather than risk being alone you decide to have your way. Now I am not talking about married couples so don't think for one moment about leaving your husband or wife. I am talking about single people who are in a relationship they know God has not sanctioned.

I have found myself in that situation on a couple of occasions. I know what it is like to want to try and make something work and at every turn see it not working. At some point you have to come to the realization that this is not what God wants for me. This is true sacrifice. When you can give up something that you want because you know God doesn't want you to have it you have exhibited true sacrifice.

It doesn't take much to give up something you don't want. But when you can relinquish something you have deep desire for and have the faith to know that God can replace it, you have shown a sign of spiritual maturity that God promises to reward. When you give up anything for his sake he will give you double for your trouble. When you tell the woman you can't see her anymore because you love Jesus more, he will give you beauty for ashes. When you give up the man you can see for the Jesus you can't see he will replace the tears with joy.

We get a better feel for why she let God do the joining when we read what God says about building a family. Psalm 127:1 says, "Except the LORD build the house, they labor in vain that build it." If God does not put it together it is like a man building a house on sand. When the storms come it will not be able to withstand the elements a storm brings with it.

But when a man builds a family on the solid foundation of the Rock of Jesus no matter what elements beat against the house it shall not prevail. When the enemy comes in like a flood the LORD shall build up a barrier against it. It is always better to build according to the specifications God gives. We may see people in the church who overlooked the counsel of God and decided to do things their way. It may even seem as if everything is going well when they walk into the church holding hands.

But what you may not be able to witness is the bitter argument that took place in route to the church. You cannot see the hatred that has grown in the heart of the couple that has permeated itself into the minds of the children. It is something that doesn't manifest itself to the naked eye until we one day see the woman walking in the church not holding the hand of he husband but the hands of her children.

I am not God nor do I pretend to know everything but I do know that those who do not learn from life's history are doom to repeat it. Many may say my relationship is not like that. My man is getting close to coming to Jesus. Some men may say my lady is about to turn the corner.

The Bible says the heart is deceitfully wicked. Who can know it? Well I only know one who can truly know the heart of man. Be very careful when you begin to think you know someone. I say again be very careful. Proverbs 3:5-6 says, "Trust in the LORD with all thine heart; and lean not unto thine own understanding. In all thy ways acknowledge him, and he shall direct thy paths."

SEVEN
WHERE ARE YOU?

...In that day seven women
shall take hold of one man... (Isaiah 4:1)

The gap between the rich and the poor in society seems to be widening every day. The distance between those that have and those that don't is increasing at a breakneck pace. However, that is nothing in comparison to the gap that has been created between available single men and available single women. There are several reasons the ratio of men to women has drastically changed over the past few decades. Since I have an evangelistic heart I want to begin by dealing with the ratio of all men and women because all are potential Christians. Every day people are turning from their life of sin and disobedience and giving their lives to Christ. So to just touch on the ratio in the House of God might misconstrue the statistics.

One of the reason the ratio of women to men has become disproportionate is more men are incarcerated today than any time in this nation's history. A myriad of reasons have caused despair in the lives of many men in America and thus have created a mind-set that has ultimately left them behind prison bars. Now you see why I had to look at the one-sided numbers from an entire society standpoint.

The reason I did is because there are many single Christian men who are stuck in this country's prison system. I love these brothers with all my heart, but I have not met one single lady who is willing to go there looking for her future mate. See I might not be able to see the heart of a man but I am part of a ministry that believes in prison outreach.

Therefore, I know for a fact that there are many men who have been committed crimes and later come to Christ for forgiveness. And I have no intention on judging their sincerity anymore than the guy walking the streets. However, though they are saved their geographical position creates a major problem for single Christian women.

Second, there are many men who are deceased. Men are dying at a much faster pace than women. They are dying of natural causes more frequently than women. They are dying of Aids, heart failure, cancer, and a host of other reasons. But men are dying at a much quicker rate than women are. Finally, more men than ever have chosen an alternative lifestyle of homosexuality. As unfortunate as this may be it is true. Let me just say to all the men and women who feel they have been born a lesbian or homosexual. If you truly feel you were born this way then be "born again." This has also created an unnecessary unbalance in potential mates for women.

Now I wanted to use my final example for the non-Christian men but as I stated previously I cannot see a man's heart. Moreover, these men seem have found their way to the church anyway. The House of God has become a haven for picking up women. I know some of you may find that shocking but it is quite true. This is why everyone especially women need to memorize a list of probing questions to ask anyone who approaches them

Everyone that has a hint of holiness is not necessarily holy. One of the main problems especially in today's contemporary church is you can learn how to act holy. You don't have to have one teaspoon of the Holy Spirit and learn how to speak tongues. You can learn when to stand and when to sit down. You learn when to shout and when to be silent. If one pays attention during one sermon he or she can pick up church protocol and go home and have perfected by the following Sunday. I know I am not lying because I seen some award-winning performances by people who don't have the slightest clue who Jesus Christ is.

They come in and give the performance of a lifetime with hopes of attracting the attention of a select few. They walk right out of the church and remove all the religious regalia and revert right back to the devil they really are. 2 Corinthians 11:13-14 says, "For such are false apostles, deceitful workers, transforming themselves into the apostles of Christ. And no marvel; for Satan himself is transformed (transforms himself) into an angel of light."

There's your text proof because I know many were thinking I was making it up. But believe me when I tell you Satan has definitely found his way into the House of God. He is no longer just waiting outside because he can't stand the sight of a cross. But he has found a comfortable spot on the pew directly beside you. My brethren understand that the Bible is not only up to date but also way ahead.

DISCERNING SPIRIT

These people are have no desire to please God and prove to be nothing more than liabilities in the church. If they are truly Christians they use God's grace as a crutch for a carnal life. God talks about such a people in Revelations 2 and calls them Nicolaitans. He says he hates this group of people. They used Christian liberty as an opportunity for self-indulgence and immorality. Bottom line is there are many people inside and outside the church we will meet who do not have our best interest at heart.

We are commanded to be of the world but not in the world. So to give any insight into where we can possibly find a mate we must see opportunity all over the world. Before I forget I want to be sure I pass this little tidbit on to you. There will be people who will attempt to come into your life for where you are right now. They will study you and with selfish ambitions determine you would be an asset to their life. It will be purely for what you can do for them.

On the other hand, there will be people who will see you as a gift from God and envision the possibilities of what the two of you could do for each other. They will seek to be an asset in your life and you in their life. I thought this was important enough to get out. I don't care if it fits at this particular time but I felt it necessary to give to you now.

There will be times God speaks to your spirit and forewarns you about a situation. Always move on what you have been given by God and don't concern yourself with what he didn't give you. God gives details as needed. Deuteronomy 29:29 says, "The secret things belong unto the LORD our God: but hose things which are revealed belong unto us and to our children for ever, that we may do all the words of this law." Do you see what I mean when I say God has things he reveals but things he doesn't. But what he does reveal is not only for us but also for our children forever. Don't just run past that without thinking. That is a Selah moment.

A moment to pause and think about what you just read. The choosing of a mate is so important because there are things that God may not finish in our generation that he will finish in our children's generation. You must understand God is not a creature of time nor does time

stop his plans. When we die God will still be doing God business. When we listen to God it has a tendency to short-circuit problems. They're a many men and women who are experiencing all types of abusive behavior in a marriage God tried to steer theme clear of. There are women who share homes with professing Christian men who view physical abuse as foreplay. There are men who are experiencing the abuse of a woman who views it as women's liberation.

More than fifty percent of this country's marriages are feeling the effects of some form of abuse. Christian marriages unfortunately are not immune to these statistics. While the Christian marriage should be a snapshot of holiness, some are taking on the form of iniquity. Some of these problems have come to fruition during the tenure but many were problems that were evident before the wedding day.

It is just a fact that some people are victims of domestic violence. That doesn't necessarily mean they were the perpetrator or were they the initial victim. They may simply have been spectators witnessing a parent or guardian engage in this ungodly behavior. Some men were in homes where they heard their father say something like "you are going to make me slap you" right before he committed the actual act. He now justifies his behavior because of what he saw and by what he feels is the woman's fault.

It is noteworthy to understand that our society pumps up our men to be a man but leaves out the godly portion. They teach boys to be a real man and don't let them see you cry. But my Bible says Jesus wept. If my LORD and Savior can cry then I know I can. Ecclesiastes 7:9 says, "Be not hasty in thy spirit to be angry: for anger resteth in the bosom of fools." You see men usually never have the opportunity to emote so anger festers inside for years. We spend years in the environment with people we can't beat. We one day find ourselves in a relationship with a weaker vessel and all the pent up anger begins to come out.

Ephesians 4:26 says, "Be ye Angry, And Sin Not: let not the sun go down you're your wrath." The Bible clearly commands us to be angry. Many of you may not have been aware of this. However, we are allowed briefly held righteous indignation as long as it doesn't lead to sin. This is used in the correct way can be an outlet which allows the steam to be released and prevent further destruction. Men who refuse to release in this way may find themselves releasing in another.

This is why is important ladies that you take time to delve into the mind and heart of a man and not just focus on what is coming out of his mouth. I here people in the church repeat over and over that Christians need balance in their lives. The people who utter this phrase usually mean we need to be able to be churchy one moment and blend in the world the next. But there is a price to pay for doing the latter. When I think of balance, I think of reading and studying God's word and then living out what I read. That's a balanced Christian life.

Those who can do this are truly outliers. An outlier is a statistical term that denotes a data point that is located far from the rest of the data. Far from the rest of the data is the key here. Not always trying to fit in with the crowd. Balance that is defined by attempting a high wire act of living for God one minute and living for Satan the next minute is dangerous proposition.

Men or women who attempt to live this sort of life put themselves in harm's way of trouble they could easily avoid. If you are truly ready for a relationship and you are a child of God why would you ever want to roll the dice with the devil? Don't get me wrong because I am all for exposure. I am behind you one hundred percent if you say we must expand our horizons. I agree and that's why God let me write this book.

However, we must keep our head on a swivel during the dating game. I don't mean to offend anyone but that is what many people you come in contact with will think this is. They will think this is just a big game of chess and God making the moves. How sadly mistaken they are and I'll tell you why. You ask any happily married Christian couple to explain how they met and they are apt to tell you it was the hand of God bringing them together. I'll give them that and agree. But tell me this who's decision was it for them to stay together? Whose decision was it to propose marriage? Whose decision was it to accept the proposal?

God has never taken our freedom to choose and he never will. I look back at the relationships I've had, and I know for a fact some of those connections were divinely inspired. That's right, God connections if you will. Yet, I sit here righting this book a single man. God will speak to your spirit and tell you to go or he'll tell you to stay.

GLEAN THE RIGHT FIELD

But the final decision will ultimately rest in the palm of your hands. The Bible says Ruth just happened to find herself in a field Boaz owned. She didn't know it but she happened to find herself gleaning there. She goes home and after telling her mother-in-law Naomi where she gleaned, she receives earthly advice. So here is a poor Moabite girl gleaning in a rich man's field.

Couple this with godly advice from a wiser woman. There is still one thing that needs to be done. Ruth must act on what she knows and what she has heard. She knows who field she has access to and has heard from a godly lady. Psalm 62:11 says, "God hath spoken once; twice have I heard this." Two witnesses for Ruth yet she still has to make a decision. When you get a moment take time and read or re-read the entire book of Ruth.

What you find out is her decision was not just some gas in the wind. It wasn't something that would pass in a moment. She was making a history making decision. Ruth by making the correct decision to follow her heart and Naomi's advice would find herself in the direct lineage of our LORD and Savior Jesus Christ.

She would end up owning the same field she was gleaning in. I cannot overemphasize the importance of our decision-making when it comes to having or not having a mate. I say not having because there are Christians who don't and are not going to get married. This decision will have nothing to do with coming in contact with suitable mates. It will be a voluntary decision they will make and there is nothing wrong with that. As Paul would say some have the gift and some don't.

Let's talk about discerning who may or may not be potential mate material. Christians should truly seek to date only Christians. I don't have any wiggle room to play with in making that statement. The decision will be totally up to you and I'll leave it at that. Now let's take a look at the three types of man and this includes men and women.

The first type of man is called a natural man. The natural man is one who is alive physically but dead spiritually. His mind and flesh work hand in glove fulfilling all it's lustful desires. Whatever the flesh desires it gets and all the memories of that sinful life are stored in the mind. This is also called an unsaved man or sinner. No disrespect intended but this is all Bible.

The second type of man is a carnal man. The carnal man is alive physically and spiritually. He is a "born again" believer. The problem is he still harbors all the sinful acts that occurred while a natural man. So he has accepted Christ as Savior but still has the propensity to fall into sin. He hates it but just can't win the war over his flesh.

The third and final man is a spirit man. The spirit man is dead physically, alive spiritually, and the mind is governed by the spirit. The spirit man has crucified the flesh and has allowed Christ to be Savior but has also allowed him to become LORD.

That's a quick synopsis of the three types of men in the world. Now the world may see more than three but God only sees three. When there is conflict between the God and the world it is always better to take God's side.

When you meet a man or woman that person will fall into one of the three categories I just described. There will be natural men who will swear to you on a stack of Bibles they are saved. They will look you directly in your face and never blink and tell you God is first in their life.

If this is the situation you find yourself in and you feel your spirit telling you to run then run. However, if you have a kind spot in your heart and you seek to see manifested proof before running there is the only thing I know to ask you. Since meeting the person in what direction has he/she been taking leading you? If the knowing the person is taking you closer to God, then they are of God. If knowing the person is taking closer to Satan then they're not of God.

I can't put it any simpler than that. People who have a heart for God will have it coming out of their pores. No matter what environment they are in the glory of God will always shine. Especially, if they are in the midst of the unsaved. If you remember when Peter denied Jesus three times every person who accused him said pretty much the same thing. They said you were with that Jesus. Once you have been with Jesus the residue will always be on you. If you spend any significant period of time studying, praying, and attending church if you even backslide, people will still know you have been with the LORD.

It is impossible to have a relationship with God and not talk about it. When the love of God is gets down in the deep crevices of your heart you won't be able to keep your mouth shut about him. It will get to the point where it becomes part of your everyday language. You will be making biblical references to earthly matters.

It will become unconscious but it will make perfect sense. Don't believe this hogwash about turning God in one environment and then turning him off in another. Show me a Christian who can do this and you are showing me hypocrite and a liar. I am not saying you couldn't intelligently hold a conversation about math, science, politics, history, or sports and refrain from saying the name Jesus. That is not what I am saying at all. What I am saying is the Holy Spirit can put godly words right in your mouth which prove to perfect for the discussed topic.

Some will understand exactly what I am attempting to delineate. Others will just have to get in the Word of God and allow the Word of God to get into them and they'll understand. My point is you will be able to ascertain much about a person by the direction they are pulling you. Of course the key is that you will have to figure it out. I say you will because there may be time when a host of others will try to do it for you. But if you are not open to receiving this type of information you will reject it. You may even draw the conclusion people are jealous or just simply don't know him/her. This is normal and is happening as I write and as you read.

There are family and friends who can see the tail and the fork and to no avail are they able to point it out to you. I say that you just cannot show someone something they don't want to see. This is not to bash or ridicule because they may actually have more patience than some of us. Some of us just don't have time to waste with people we feel are not in our best interest.

If a man or woman cannot submit to God then what makes people think they will submit to them. I am talking to Christians here. Listen as Christians we know the work it takes to live a holy and blameless life. We know the holy sweat needed to keep ourselves in check right now in a single state. So if we look at ourselves having the divine help of the Holy Spirit and we still have issues, why in the world would we want to be with someone who has NO help?

KEEP IT IN THE FAMILY

I hope I helped someone in those previous passages. Let's take a look some of the different avenues available to meet single God-fearing men and women. To find places acceptable we also need to know what is not acceptable. Now I don't want anyone to be held hostage by my opinion. Allow your spirit to be your guide.

The Bible says in 1 Corinthians 10:23, "All things are lawful for me, but all things are not expedient: all things are lawful for me, but all things are lawful for me, but all things edify (do not build up) not." Many Christians have mini wars about where we can and cannot go.

My take on this is simply to do what verse thirty-one says and that is, "Whatsoever ye do, do all to the glory of God." Instead of focusing on where we shouldn't and start a bonfire, I will take a little time and mention some places we should.

Right off the bat I will say the House of God is an excellent place to meet a future mate. I truly believe God has a way a getting people in the right situation at the right time. I feel it happens when neither party is expecting it. It could be a fellow Christian introducing two people in an impromptu fashion. It could happen during the walk to the car before or after service. Some Christians will stand on their soapbox and talk about the fact we come to church to praise and worship God and that is true. But what in the world do they consider fellowship?

I sure hope it is defined as me hugging old ladies and shaking old men's hands. I pray it just doesn't entail me waiting until after the service and shaking the pastor's hand. It has to be more than me speaking to the greeters and ushers. Come on people and let's grow up.

Some of the healthiest marriages have been birthed before and after worship services. I agree we should never make this a primary purpose anytime we step foot in the House of God but if we never allow ourselves to be open to the fact God could make it happen we will categorize every meeting we have with the opposite sex as hello and good-bye. The best way I can think of that will allow God to work in this setting is simple.

Christian men and women should be doing this anyway, but if you are single and want to be married learn to do what I am about to say. If you want to be in the position to talk to a man or woman you would like to possibly date, then learn to be able to talk to anyone. Many Christians single, married, or whatever walk right into the God's house, take their seat and never bother getting to know the person on the right or left side of them.

And if the preacher didn't say hug your neighbor they would end up spending two to three hours professing to love God, yet never acknowledging God's people. We are commanded to be give both tablets of the Ten Commandments our undivided attention. This means God and man unconditionally.

If Christians could learn to walk into the service and speak to the elderly lady, little child, or middle-aged man with the same fervor, then when God put the future mate beside them conversation would be natural. When we allow the natural course of events to take it's over we will find not only can God make the connection he can connect you with the exact kind of person you desire. I'm talking to both men and women and I hope you hear me.

Dispense with the idea that church is not the place to find love. All we do when we deny this is cause people to view it taboo if we even talk to a person of the opposite sex for longer than five minutes. Sex and money remain the two subjects no one wants to talk about, yet everything breathing want and want in abundance. I know some don't want it and can't have but that is for another book and another time.

I desire not to make God's house a pick-up joint but people we cause so many problems when we make people feel that church is not a place that can birth godly relationships. If more churches instituted ministries that focused on this there would be less fornicating behavior amongst the church people.

We have women coming up pregnant all around the church and no one wants to address the problem. Christians are sneaking around and many times because the saints of the old order of things refuse to grow up.

Man's tradition is not what we should teach to counteract the problem of sexual immorality in the House of God. Scripture never needs the support of man. It is man who needs the support of scripture. There are many older saints who have handcuffed the entire church by propagating the human made doctrines they lived by decades ago. Now don't get me wrong because I love and have infinite respect for the elders in the church.

But you have to give them more than long dresses, hats and no make-up if you want to quench the fiery darts Satan is throwing. Religious regalia has never and will never stop the spirit of promiscuity in a Christian's life. The Bible says that Job made a covenant with his eyes to never look lustfully at a woman. That was a wonderful covenant but why didn't he make a covenant with his mind. You can turn your head all you want to but what about your mind.

What do you do while you are still being transformed. We have to find a way to bridge the gap between what happened in the past and what is happening in the present and future. I was studying about the doctrine of first mention and discovered something quite interesting. Any time you want to get God's stance on any subject it is always smart to go back to The Old Testament. Read that portion of scripture and pay close attention how God dealt with the subject you are seeking.

HOW DOES GOD FEEL

The example I want to use is the Sabbath. The Bible says in Genesis 2:1-3 that God finished the heavens and earth (I'm paraphrasing) and rested from all the work he had done. He sanctified the day he rested on. By sanctifying the day he made it a holy or set apart. Keep following me. This was the seventh day according to verse two.

Fast-forward to today and we have made two distinct changes we have made regarding this rest day. First, we Christians consider the first day the day of rest. Why? Things changed. The events in the very next chapter were the precursor to why we now rest on day one. The second thing is we have not only changed the day but we have added to specs. We now use the day to praise and worship. The verses I previously spoke of never told us to do that. Understand when I say we I am including the men in the book of Acts. The change began there and we have been following their lead ever since.

But did God rest on the first day? Did God command us to praise and worship him on the first day? God sanctified the day or set the day apart from other days and ceased from his finished work. My point is the first mention gave us a God's character of what should be done on this particular day, but because when sin entered the world it perpetuated a change. Adam's sin changed everything and because the Christ was needed a new order was instituted, when he died, was buried, and rose on Sunday morning. The Christian family then deem this the Lord's Day. Let's probe a little deeper. Did Jesus Christ ever contradict God's first mentioned word of Genesis and command us to worship on the first day?

Sin caused God's rest to be broken so the seventh day is no longer THE day of rest either. Some follow this according to the strict letter of the law, but if you decided to rest and take off a day of work and rest, then get called into work because of a crisis only you can fix the rest day has just become a workday again.

I am trying not to get overly analytical, but what I am trying to get the church to understand is we cannot keep burying our heads in the sand and continue using our old man made specs. It is important that we let God's Word transform our tradition and not let tradition become the standard. Things have changed and the devil has moved his evil from the garden to the church.

God had a plan before he slithered into picture. Therefore, we because we are of God we should have had a plan as well. We didn't and Satan has infiltrated his plan with relative ease. And the result has caused havoc amongst the people of God.

It is total and blatant disobedience when we not only are engaging in sexual interludes but we are not even protecting ourselves when we do. You cannot deal with this type of devil with long dresses and hymn notes. You are going to have to find another anecdote for this spiritual disease. It took a while for me to understand what people meant by fighting fire with fire until I saw a California forest fire. The firefighters would actually start smaller fires in spots to cut the major fire off.

If we want to beat Satan at his own game we must create a way for people to not be guilt ridden if they find themselves seeking to date a fellow member of the church. Instead let's educate them on how to conduct them as they matriculate through the dating process. We assume that people know. That is another problem because they are proving they don't. What we know is what we were taught in the world. Thus, re-training is necessary.

Everything we do has to be preceded by the preposition RE. Bringing guilt to and condemnation is not what the church should be doing. I know some people are saying no one is making them feel guilty, but believe me when I tell you there are people in the very church you are attending who frown relationships between members that don't end in marriage a week after the initial meeting. I think one of the reasons is because of our carnal thinking. We assume saints cannot date without bringing sex into the fold. This accusatory attitude ends up running the couple directly into the bedroom.

They feel ostracized by the very people who should be supporting them. The only arms they find to run into ends up being there own and that becomes of recipe for disaster. This is where good solid teaching would be better served. But some would say if they are not going to marry immediately it is better to sever than to serve.

REMEMBER FIRST LOVES

I have probably spent too much time on this but I feel it necessary since I am talking to Christians. There could be some outstanding and holy relationships developed if we all would put on our thinking caps and see the glass half full instead of half empty. I cannot think of a more productive situation than to find a potential mate in the House of God and then feel totally comfortable about discussing that same relationship with godly folk in the church. Nevertheless, when you attempt to please everybody you sometimes find that you please nobody.

Beloved, we must develop better spiritual bonds and trust with one another. If God has put something together who are we to determine when or how it should grow. Let God have an opportunity to do his perfect work in his people's lives. The thing fellow saints should do is to support the entire work of God. This is extremely important not just for what I have been discussing but for every thing we have been tasked to do in the House of the LORD.

I have found that theaters, art galleries, museum, and bookstores are excellent places to meet people of eclectic taste. I feel one of the major misnomers of the Christian people is that we are boring, aloof, and sad. I want to dispel that myth right now. We are some of the most inviting people that anyone would ever want to meet.

More important is that we understand that fact ourselves. When didn't come into this world saved. There were interests we had and acted upon during our time of disobedience to God. We must now harness those interests and find a way to glorify God with some of those same interests.

Many of us had a passion for theater and plays prior to becoming "born again." We should not abandon that interest but rather change the type of plays we attend. This opens up the same mating possibilities that were available before. We should now seek to be in the company of like-minded people. We must also realize there are no clear cut remedies to finding a future mate but we can increase the possibilities of a fruitful and healthy tie.

Remember Paul says we should be not conformed but be transformed by the renewing of our mind. As we allow God to change our thinking we will find that instead of fellowshipping in unhealthy environments and open ourselves up to demonic evil, we should find different places for socialization. As I previously stated I am not going to try and place anyone under bondage by naming places we shouldn't go. But, I will say that if a place you desire to visit decreases your chances of meeting a godly mate then you should give serious consideration to not going.

Listen there are places that the people of the world deem to be unacceptable to visit. There are hole-in-the-wall places unsaved people wouldn't dare be caught in, yet many Christians push the envelop of grace and use the "balance theory" to support there idea.

Now I don't want my men to think I am getting on their case but make no mistake about it, God expects us to fulfill the role of leadership. This begins from the on-set and not when the union is developed under the canopy of marriage. I am truly from the old school of thought and believe in courting a lady.

So we must always be cognizant about the places we find ourselves visiting. Things have changed so much over the years that we need to beware of the differences in the expectations and desires of women. We must be like the men God describes in 1 Chronicles 12:32 when he says, "The children of Issachar, *which were men* that had understanding of the times." These men were always growing and maturing regardless of the change in the land.

Change is inevitable but when you sow change you will reap the benefits of what you sow. I am not a fighting man but when I was growing up in the streets of New York I found out very early that if you are going to get into a fight it would be to your advantage if you get the first lick in.

Especially, it the opponent was bigger than I was. We are in a spiritual battle and when we put ourselves in the position to succeed the chances for success will surely increase. Another place I find to be a healthy environment for meeting people is the bookstore. Men should desire women who not only are Christian but women who are consistently finding ways to grow. The Bible says we are love the LORD with all our heart, soul, strength, and mind.

If I am commanded to love God in those areas then I need to always be exercising those areas. 3 John 2 says, "Beloved, I wish (pray) above all things that thou mayest prosper and be in health, even as thy soul prospereth. A Christian who doesn't seek to expand his or her horizons in all facets of life is disobeying the Word of God. Do you see why I constantly find myself talking about God's infallible Word? If we live our lives according to the Bible we couldn't help but prosper in the things of the LORD.

I don't know how God will work out the divine connection in your life so don't take every suggestion as gospel. I know people who were sitting on the couch and were prompted by the Holy Spirit to take a trip to the grocery store. The person had no desire for anything in the grocery store but had the desire to go. He went and found himself walking in the grocery turning down a particular isle and running into his future wife. It can happen just like that. You could meet that special person at the bus stop. It could happen during a routine check-up at the doctor or dentist's office. I assume we are getting our teeth and body's checked out on a routine basis. See I plan on giving you everything the LORD gives me. Maintaining a healthy hygienic life is critical.

My brothers understand that clean women are not attracted to men who do no take care of themselves in the hygienic area. Notice I said clean women. But the same goes for the women. Men like the hands and feet to be manicured at all times. We understand bad hair days happen to the best of them, but I myself find no reason for not taking care of your teeth, hands, and feet. That's my opinion and I am sure there are some who will disagree. God Bless You.

You would think these things wouldn't have to be said but trust me they do. There are folks who believe giving the life to Christ means letting themselves go totally and completely. This is pure nonsense and I hope I am doing something to put an end to it right now. We are expected to love God with all our strength so take care of your body. I won't delve into this too much because I spoke of this in an earlier chapter, but saints please do your very best to maintain the upkeep on the one and only body you will have on this side of eternity.

I have recently been hearing about an internet dating service especially for Christians. I don't want to create any stir regarding this so just chalk this up to as my humble opinion. I truly don't find anything wrong with using this vehicle to meet someone. I feel the positives are that you can control how far you want things to go before you ever meet or see the person.

You can develop camaraderie before the first date. As a man you can find the type of woman you are physically attracted to and then build from there. You allow yourself the opportunity to find out where they stand in the spiritual belief. Of course as with the conventional meeting you have to be able to discern whether the person is being truthful with you.

This method is more profitable in my opinion for the ladies. You can decipher whether a man is right for you and not have the hassle of frivolous dates. Always realize there are pros and cons to any service that fall along these lines. There are some things you should always do to protect yourself. Women should always be careful regardless of the medium used for dating. Until you are truly comfortable never give out your phone number or address.

With the advent of email you now possess another way to keep communication lines open. By the same token don't assume every guy is a seeking to harm you in a physical or emotional way. Men and women who are single and actively looking for a mate need to understand it may not happen on the first try. This is why you must do as Proverbs 4:23 says, "Guard your heart." We also should refrain from actually going on a date until the conversation has made you feel comfortable. But we must not expect to strike gold with the first person we see.

The web site is just an icebreaker just as meeting someone in passing would be. You see them and they see you and physical attraction opens the door but once you walk in you may not like the scenery. That is part of the dating process. Therefore, you should always maintain you class and integrity. And believe me saints those two qualities are steadily becoming the most important on the list of the things people seek in a mate.

It is not a given to assume attractive people have attractive character. This will take a little investigating to deduce. But however long it takes it will be well worth it. I just recently read a newspaper article about a woman's quest to be engaged in six months. She has set up her own website in hopes of finding her future husband. I applaud her zeal but must caution that when you put a time limit on something like this you open yourself up to choosing someone based on the timetable rather than love.

This is can lead to having to deal with things one never expected. A person can be so entrenched in finding that potential mate their vision and judgment becomes cloudy. One becomes so focused on their deadline that they completely miss the fact the man or woman is not the one. I have heard stories of Christian women slashing tires and throwing fits in the workplace in regards to a man. And I have heard of Christian men staking out the homes of women for the sole purpose of catching them cheating. These are issues none of us in the family of God need to have.

We have too many other devils to fight than to have to deal with immature behavior such as this. Let the world engage in those things and we then in turn show them the godly way. Amen.

REAL MEN STAND UP

Ezekiel 22:30 says, "...I sought for a man among them, that should make up the hedge, and stand in the gap before me for the land, that I should not destroy it: but I found none."

This is especially for the Christian all over the world. I am going to use that scripture as a pre-text to challenge you to put away your promiscuous ways. I am not merely talking about casual sex with various partners. I am talking about your unwillingness to do the right thing when you know you have the right woman. This promiscuity doesn't have anything to do with actually having sex.

While I am here I will repeat what I said in an earlier chapter regarding masturbation. Many men use this wicked act to hold women hostage and it is wrong. They try and portray a man who has it together sexually when in fact he doesn't. He uses the woman for times when he wants company but internally knows he has no intentions of marrying her.

Let me tell you that God is not happy with this arrangement you have cut out for yourself. And to make matters worse you are allowing the devil to gain a major foot hole in your life. He uses this evil to deceive you twice. The act leads you into thinking you will get intimacy and you don't. But the main thing it does it put friction between you and God. Let me add my own extra tidbit on how he scars you. A many men and women will look down their self-righteous noses at gay and lesbian people.

But remember this the next time you decide to engage in this deplorable act of self-gratification. Who is in the room with you? Dare I say you since it is self-gratification you as a man or you as a woman have just engaged in the very act you criticize another group for doing. That's one of those things that make you say, *Hmmm*.

If you are not going to marry the woman then let her know. Remember you reap what you sow. If you are not sure she is the one then by all means give her the opportunity to make the decision if she wants to hang around. I know this can work the other way as well, but more often than not it doesn't.

God says in Ezekiel he sought a man. The omnipresent God of the universe sought a man and found none. God is still seeking men who will make up the difference he cannot. Yes the woman is saved, sanctified, and filled with the Holy Ghost, but God wants the earth overflowing with godly people.

Therefore, he needs godly men to form godly unions with godly women to produce godly seeds. That is it in a nutshell. This is for both the men and the women. You must understand that the devil has no new tricks. Everything he does is just repackaged and resold to society. We need to quit buying what he is selling because nothing has changed. The name of the evil may change but the essence of it will always remain the same. He seeks to destroy the plan and purposes God has for our lives.

When were unsaved and not thinking about God at all he whispers in our ear don't worry there's no hurry. We buy into this lie. For the Bible says the time for salvation is now and don't forget it is always now. So what does he do now that we are saved? He comes at us with the exact same lie but in a different gown.

We know we are with the person we should be with and he whispers that we've got time. He tells us to take it easy and live our life. But it's not our life. It belongs to God now. Jesus redeemed us with his blood on Calvary and we are not our own. God wants a godly seed that this world might not go completely to hell. We play right into his hand when we procrastinate in areas we already know what to do.

This can be in the area of tithing, church participation, offerings, ministry building or whatever else we know we should be doing. He even played with my mind about writing this book. He told me many times nobody would read it and nobody would care. Well let us take a look and see what Jesus says about Satan in John 8:44-45 when he rebuked the Pharisees.

He says, "Ye are of *your* father the devil, and the lusts of your father ye will do. He was a murderer from the beginning, and abode not in the truth, because there is no truth in him. When he speaketh a lie, he speaketh of his own: for he is a liar, and the father of it. And because I tell *you* the truth, ye believe me not." Jesus could put you in your place when he wanted to.

That's why I think people are crazy when they try and portray our LORD as a weak and timid man. Not so my brethren as you can see from those two scriptures. But re-read it and notice that Jesus says the devil is a liar. It not that he just speaks and lies to not be truthful but he cannot be truthful. It does not matter what he says it is a lie pure and simple. So you ask how do I know when he is lying to me? I'm glad you asked.

You know when you conjure up in your little mind any plan that is not in line with God's word. You know what you should be doing in regards to that woman and you don't do it. You know what you should be doing in regards to that man and you don't do it. These are the basic signs that you are not being obedient to God. You will have to wait for the next book in order for me to go deeper than that. However, your disobedience will only hinder your life. Look what God says in Proverbs 19:21, "There are many devices (plans/schemes) in a man's heart; Nevertheless, the counsel of the LORD, THAT shall stand."

God will let you act like a fool all your heart desires. You can try and play the woman for a fool until your heart is content. You can disobey what he commands you to do as a godly man or woman. But in the end God's counsel will come to pass. I am not saying God will find a way to ensure you marry that man or woman. That is far from what I am saying. But what he will do is ensure that jilted individual will end up receiving double for their trouble.

And you will be standing there looking stupid. The same goes for not doing what he says financially. You will tithe one way or another. It may not be to the church but you will begin to see things in your life break down that never broke down before. You variable expenses will begin to shoot through the roof. Everything from the washing machine to your own physical body will start breaking down one by one. Why? Because you are under a curse.

I have learned that God is not going to bulldoze his way into your life. He wants to be invited in. He wants to tabernacle with you. To tabernacle is to dwell or take up residence. This is what God truly desires to do with every Christian man and woman. It is then will you really begin to enjoy the infinite benefits of being saved.

This is why I get so annoyed by people who are constantly saying God said to me this and God said to me that. My question is why in the world should I believe you. Give me one good reason to believe God said anything to you. Never replace what is in God's Word with what anybody says. Always accept what the Bible says but that doesn't mean you have to accept what someone says the Bible says. Everybody holding a Bible and preaching are not necessarily preaching from the book they're holding.

This is why Paul was so impressed with the people from Berea in the seventeenth chapter of the book of **Acts.** After they heard Paul preach they immediately went home and searched the scriptures to ensure Paul knew what he was talking about. The Bible says they received the preaching with readiness of mind but that didn't stop them from testing the spirit. We have gotten so lazy today anybody preaching anything at anytime gets two thumbs up if he or she is holding a bible in their hand.

Remember what I am about to say if you don't remember anything else you've read. If God didn't say it is it really truth? This includes what I or any other authors have written. Let God direct your entire life and watch the miracles he will perform. Finding the perfect person to share your life with will ultimately ride on you becoming the perfect person God wants you to be.

I didn't say a perfect but the perfect. In addition, realize that though there are no perfect people there are faithful ones. You cannot put a price tag on someone you know will come through when expected. Therefore, if you find a perfect person I would advise you to run as fast as you can. If someone is too good to be true they usually are. So what is the will of God for your life? 1 Thessalonians 4:3-4 says, "For this is the will of God *even* your sanctification, that ye should abstain from fornication (sexual impurity). That every one of you should know how to possess his vessel in sanctification and honor." God expects us to know how to live our life in a holy and godly matter.

This doesn't just mean what not to do but it also includes things we should do. Realize that God wants to control your flesh through your spirit while Satan wants to control your flesh through your mind. Therefore, building up the spirit man becomes paramount. This can only come from knowing him through his Word.

My people are destroyed for lack of knowledge: because thou hast Rejected knowledge. I will also reject thee, that thou shalt be no priest To me: seeing thou hast forgotten the law of thy God. I will also forget Thy children. (Hosea 4:6)

FLIP THE SWITCH

God expects men and women to utilize the time we have here to glorify him and not waste it with selfish ambitions. We all are diamonds in the rough waiting for someone to excavate and shine. Remember that in the parable of the talents it was person with ten, a person, with five, and a person with one. There was not a person with zero. God gives everyone talents to use for his pleasure and glory. If you're not completely happy with the relationship you have now then do something to spice it up.

Institute a date night and stick the plan. Take walks in the park or on the beach. Go on a cruise for visit a tropical island. Send your lady flowers for no reason at all. Ladies deliver flowers to your man's office if possible. Go to a coffeehouse at midnight and share a conversation about where you see the relationship going.

Break up the monotony that the hustle and bustle life brings. In other words, endeavor to make time for one another. Both parties should learn the art of listening. Read these two scriptures in Jeremiah 42:5-6, "They (God's people) said to Jeremiah, the LORD be a true and faithful witness between us, if we do not even according to all things for the which the LORD thy God shall send thee to us. Whether *it be* good, or whether *it be* evil, we will obey the voice of the LORD our God, to whom we send thee; that it may be well with us, when we obey the voice of the LORD our God."

These very same people one chapter later would be doing the exact opposite of what they promised they would do. The sad thing is nothing has changed since that time. We make promises to God and people and instead of seeking diligently to keep them, we with without any thought rescind on our own word.

It is one thing to not do what someone says, but it is blatant disobedience when you know what you should do, promise to do it, and then do the opposite. Some people would call that lying. But you didn't hear it from me. Therefore, we must learn to really hearken which includes listening and doing. And remember that listening is not waiting to talk.

Let he that hath an ear hear. Don't give your entire life the cares of the world and let them steal the relationship God blessed you with. Most importantly, always take time to pray with one another. And never chide one another in the presence of others. Don't view your differences as deal-breakers but see them as character builders. Irreconcilable differences should cause growth and not division in the godly family. Let it not be said that you can get along with everyone else of the opposite sex at work or in other venues but cannot get along with your mate or future mate. Some of us tend to want to allow the wrong people in our lives and keep the right people out. Remember Satan is still in the business of beguiling. Deuteronomy 33:25 says, "…as thy days, *so shall* thy strength *be"* so if we appear inept to the temptations of the devil, we can rest in assurance that God will be our strength in a time of weakness.

In addition, be aware of how you praise your potential mate. Some people tend to give backhanded comments that seem like praise. What they do is talk about how important you are to them by describing their success. The makes statements about how great they are give you a little credit. Subtle pride is what this is and should never go unchecked.

I truly hope I am helping someone with these words God has blessed me with. Any differences we have in personality should prove worthy in developing spiritual cohesion hopefully in all our relationships. We must learn to be patient with one another as God is patient with us. If one has an insouciant personality and another is outgoing, they must know that these differences will eventually become advantageous to their over-all relationship. There will be introverted and extroverted characters finding themselves together. No reason to be alarmed. Just use those traits as building blocks to your own individual spiritual maturity.

It will become vitally important we all learn the art of saying these four things: I was wrong, I apologize, I don't know (But I know where to find out), and I need help. Never have any trepidation about expressing your weakness or concerns to your potential mate. When we open up in this way it allows for the other person to become a part of what the person may be going through. Also, men understand that sometimes women just want to give us a hug to let us know everything is going to be okay. It's not an act of foreplay.

Gentlemen sometimes when women do these types of things they are only showing their appreciation. The foundation you lay will determine the house you will eventually build. Don't put up unnecessary fronts to prove you strength. This can backfire and have catastrophic results.

I know these are tough things to say sometimes, but it shows your strength in character and weakness. We must understand that the social aspects of life are geared to the younger generation. They have more disposable income and more time to spend it. Therefore, we old folk better learn to use ingenuity to keep the flame going in our social lives. Hallelujah.

Finally, learn the art of forgiveness. It is a lost art but it needs to be retrieved and retooled in order for any Christian to become the well-rounded saint God would have him/her to be. It is amazing to me how unforgiving Christians can be.

We have been forgiven so many times but the God of Heaven and yet we are experts as holding grudges. The thing we must understand is grudges can last for years. They have the propensity to take a physical, mental, and emotional toll on us for long periods of time. We must learn to release ourselves from these grudges.

What I have learned is when we release someone through forgiveness we actually free our own minds. You may still feel the person was wrong for what he or she did, but by forgiving them you free your own spirit.

When you take the steps to forgive them do not be surprised if they don't feel like they did anything wrong. You are not trying to get them to admit anything. The key is to free yourself from the friction that exists between you and the other party. It may behoove you to expect them to not be receptive to your act of contrition. That is absolutely fine because the last thing you want to do is have this meeting become another opportunity for salt to be poured on the womb. During the discussion do not over-talk. If one sentence is sufficient then use one.

Your mission is to apply a tourniquet to stop the bleeding of a situation the devil can and will use against you both. I have stated on many occasions when speaking that Satan comes when we are Hungry, Angry, Lonely, and Tired.

Now if you take the first letter of each of those words and put them together you get the word you should tell yourself when he comes. HALT. You may not have any control over the response of the one being forgiven but you do have control over the one doing the forgiving. Exercise that control in the spirit of love. For the love of a Christian never fails.

And always remember love is about giving not receiving. For John 3:16 says, "For God so loved the world, that he gave his only begotten Son, that whosoever believeth in him should not perish, but have everlasting life." We have no better example to follow than Almighty God himself.

EPILOGUE

I thank my Lord and Savior Jesus Christ for the opportunity to partake in the greatest call in the history of the world. The call to go into the world and preach the wonderful and glorious gospel of Jesus Christ to every creature. I take it very serious to call myself a Christian and even more serious to preach God's precious word.

"I was not prophet, neither was I a prophet's son; but I was a herdman, and a gatherer of sycamore fruit: And the Lord took me as I followed the flock, and the Lord said unto me, Go, prophesy unto my people Israel." (Amos 7:14-15). I can attest to these words of the prophet Amos. I was not looking to preach nor was I part of any pedigree of preachers. I was minding my own business or yet Satan's business and God took me. Hallelujah.

It's because of this call I humbly come before God each and every day seeking the wisdom and spiritual discernment to do his will on earth as it is in heaven. It is quite overwhelming to be a follower of the flock one day and be called to lead the flock the next as the prophet Amos so eloquently stated. To pull this off takes a special anointing from God not from man. Through the grace, mercy, and favor of God I have been able to complete the written requirements for this call. However, the call to lead any of God's precious children requires discipline, humility, faith, love, patience, meekness, kindness, determination, zeal. peace, and joy.

I intend on fulfilling this call to the best of my ability and with prayer I know God will never leave me nor forsake me as I press toward the mark for the prize.

With the advent of television the church seems to be stuck in an entertainment mode. This troubles me because the Gospel of our Lord Jesus Christ is not about entertainment. This is about relationship.

We must never confuse our call, mission, and purpose with the world's program. We are the called out ones. We are not supposed to be doing things according to the world's system but according to God's system. The church could really go somewhere if we would come out from among them (world) and be separate. Not disconnect ourselves because we must evangelize, but not allow them to affect us.

The church should be a spiritual cancer affecting the world and laying a foundation as an example to what God would have his world to look like. When we get on television and preach everything except the pure unadulterated Gospel of Jesus Christ we prostitute the word for our own selfish gain. The Christians lose, the unsaved lose, the preacher loses and God's program is rendered ineffective.

Note I said I said is rendered ineffective. God never loses and if he has to let an entire generation die out he will but his word will not return to him void. Either we play by his rules or He'll rise up a jackass to speak. Either way God's plan, which was laid before the foundation of the world will come to pass.

When we preach a financial prosperity gospel, faith gospel. healing gospel, blessing gospel, or any other gospel, we are preaching another gospel.

"But though we, or an angel from heaven, preach any other gospel unto you than that which we have preached unto you, let him be accursed. As we said before, so say I now again, If any man preach any other gospel unto you than that ye have received, let him be accursed." (Galatians 1:8-9).

This was so important Paul repeated it and God never repeats Himself unless it is of the utmost importance. These are scriptures that our generation today has failed to over look. We preach promises of name it and claim it and that is not God's way.

When we pray to God we should be praying and petitioning God according to his will not our will. For he know what we have need of before we pray. So why pray? He needs us to beseech him to enter into our affairs. But our affairs must line up with his WORD and not our desires.

We deceive people and give false hopes when we preach another gospel other than the Gospel of Christ. We sell false hopes to build our ministries and make names for ourselves. This is ought not to be. Jesus said, "If I be lifted up I will draw ALL men unto me." He did not say if men be lifted up. We all should be men and women who seek to lift up the name of Jesus so the lost can come. We should be saints who seek to only glorify the name of Jesus at any and all cost. Never seeking fame or fortune, but only the saving of lost souls. I must declare that I am appalled and embarrassed as a Christian when I hear some of the propaganda that is being peddled as the Gospel.

I will spend the rest of my life preaching God's word which when received is able to save the soul of the sinner. God's word is true and need not be added to nor deleted from to be effective.

Sadly in the case of many of the false teachings of financial prosperity, the people who seem to always be in lack are the flock of God. The preachers however are consistently selling more books, buying bigger private planes, bigger homes, more cars, building bigger churches, and making more money at the sheep's expense.

This must stop. I am not against the prosperity of God's people. I am against the outright prostituting of God's people and Word for the self-interest of a greedy few. I say few because it is not many nor does it require many to spoil the vine.

"But, beloved, we are persuaded better things, of you, and things that accompany salvation though we thus speak. For God is not unrighteous to forget your work and labor of love, which ye have showed toward his name, in that ye have ministered to the saints, and do minister." (Hebrews 6:9-10).

This is one of my favorite scriptures and when we couple this with scriptures which call for us to evangelize the world we realize if we do what God has called us to do we won't be able to escape the blessings of the Lord.

I hear so many sermons on 3 steps to this, 7 steps to this, and 12 steps to that. Well I have a three-step program that is ironclad and cannot fail. If God's people want to see their lives blessed this is all they have to do.

First, Love the Lord thy God with all thy heart, and with all thy soul, and with all thy strength, and with thy entire mind. If you are to do this you must exercise each of these areas.

To exercise the heart where the spirit resides one must meditate on the Word of God day and night. For blessed is the man that studies God word continually. He shall be like a tree planted by the rivers of water that brings forth his fruit in his season; his leaf also shall not wither; and whatsoever he doeth shall prosper.

The soul and mind are where our emotions, feelings, and intellect reside. We must know about different things of the world and not be of the world. We must study God's word and know what's going on in other aspects of life. I always say, "I don't know a lot about one thing but I know a little about a lot of things." We must have our finger on the pulse of many subjects in order to evangelize in all circles.

Our strength can be viewed as our bodies. The Bible says bodily exercise profiteth little but it didn't say it didn't profit at all. We must take care of our selves. Our bodies are the temples of the Holy Spirit and we must treat them as such or they will fail.

Second, Love thy neighbor as thyself. The key here is to Love thyself first. We cannot possibly love (agape) others unless we love ourselves. There are many Christians who do not love themselves. They are saved yet because they don't have the possessions the world deems as successful (House, Car, Husband, Wife, Wealth, Children, Etc.) they feel their lives are inadequate.

This is part of the misconception that false preaching can do. Spiritual maturity is not based on the size of your portfolio or bank account. When we truly understand what God has wrought for us in redemption we will walk in the newness of life and experience the peace and joy that surpasses all understanding.

"Beloved, I wish above all things that thou mayest prosper and be in health, even as thy soul prospereth." (3 John 2). God did not call us out of darkness into his marvelous as a holy nation and a royal priesthood to have us live in lack. However, we must read the word daily to know what God has purposed for our lives.

Third, make it your life's mission to win souls for the Lord. For he who does is called wise in the Book of Proverbs. I sincerely believe the Word of God and ALL it's promises. Therefore, I study it and meditate on it and pray according to the plan of God.

Joshua 1:8 states, "This Book of the Law shall not depart out of thy mouth; but thou shalt meditate therein day and night, that thou mayest observe to do according to ALL that is written therein: for then thou shalt make thy way prosperous, and then thou shalt have good success."

This literally means that if God's children live their lives according to the Bible they couldn't stop the blessings of the Lord from coming upon their life. It is a guarantee that you will be blessed in the city and in the field. You could only be the head and never the tail. You could not help but be abundantly blessed with all spiritual and earthly blessings from God.

"While we look not at the things which are seen, but at the things which are not seen: for the things which are seen are temporal; but the things which are not seen are eternal." (2 Corinthians 4:18). The reason many Christians are not seeing the manifestation of God's presence in their lives is because they are looking for it.

Jesus said seek first the Kingdom of God and ALL it's righteousness and ALL these things shall be added unto thee. What are THESE things? Clothing, food, shelter, wives, husbands, and jobs. Jesus says God has clothed the Lilies and taken care of the birds will he not do more for you. We are his workmanship created unto good works. God would be a liar if he did not take care of his own and he would not lie about taking care of his own any more than any good parent would about taking care of his/her child.

John 3:16 states, "For God so Loved the world he gave his only begotten Son, that whosoever believeth in him should not perish, but have everlasting life."

John 10:10 states, "The thief cometh not, but for to steal, and to kill, and to destroy: I (Jesus) AM come that they (God's Children) might have life, and that they might have it more abundantly."

Everlasting means lasting forever or eternal and abundantly means affording a plentiful supply. What more could a Christian want other than a Life lasting forever with a plentiful supply. This of course is a question only true Christians can answer. After hearing that someone took an unofficial and informal survey of a group of professing Christians this is what I learned. This referred to Christians in America only. Though unofficial it gives us a glimpse at why many Christians never can make godly decisions. Upon learning this I almost fell out of my seat.

Ten percent of professing Christians cannot be found anywhere. They are not found on any church membership rolls. Twenty percent of professing Christians NEVER attend church. How can one say he or she is a Christian and NEVER get the inclination to visit the House of God? Twenty-five percent NEVER pray. The main reason or better yet excuse is the lack of time. God gives a man a twenty-four day and man cannot in turn give him a few minutes to thank him for it. Unbelievable. Thirty percent NEVER read the Bible. How in the world can you say you believe in the God of the Bible and not read the Bible of the God? This in spite of the fact that the Bible is the usually the best selling book on an annual basis. It is purchased and NEVER read by many people.

Forty percent NEVER give money such as tithes or freewill offerings to the church. Christian people blesses by God with a job, career, and finances but do not feel led to give back to further the gospel. Fifty percent NEVER attend a Sunday evening service. These folks find no interest in giving up any time unless it is convenient for them. Sixty percent NEVER give to world or missionary causes. This group doesn't think what goes on in other countries has anything to do with them. Beloved, Christians are all over the world and regardless of their geographical location they are part of the House of God.

Seventy-five percent NEVER work in the various ministries of the church. These are pew sitters who, by their continued disobedience of refusing to serve, try to kill the other twenty-five percent who actually do. Eighty-five percent NEVER attend a mid-week service or Bible class. This contingent is too weary after work to spare a couple of hours to learn line-by-line and precept-by-precept scripture they definitely use. Ninety-five percent NEVER have led a person to Christ. But that's okay because one hundred percent think they are going to heaven. I know we are saved by faith and not by works but these are works that should come when our faith kicks in.

This is why I feel it necessary to get back to preaching the good old fashion gospel. If it could save a wretched man like Paul and spawn a ministry which is forever stitched in our consciousness then why isn't it good enough for today's sinner. God doesn't owe us anything else. We were disconnected from him and HE took it upon himself to reconcile us back to himself. Not so we could achieve cars, houses, and money but so that HE could once again enjoy fellowship with his creation.

We are here for God. This is what should accompany the Gospel today. He will never leave us or forsake us. This is a promise written in blood and sweat. The movie, *The Passion of the Christ*, shows a small percentage of what Jesus suffered that we might have that eternal life. For Isaiah states his visage was marred more than any other man. Jesus was actually unrecognizable as he hung naked on the cross.

Why would I preach about the frivolous things the world system considers a success? It all will pass away one day but God's word will never pass away. I sincerely pray that more people will get back to doing what God commissioned us to do. He's coming back and desires that ALL men be save. Jesus alone can save the world, but Jesus can't save the world alone. He needs us to spread the word.

Muslims, Jehovah's Witnesses, Buddhist, and other false religions are taking their message to the streets in droves. Yet, Christians who know the Bible is the TRUTH refuse to display the zeal of our counterparts. We must understand that we can call Satan many things, but one thing we can NEVER call him is lazy. He is forever accusing the brethren and spreading lies because he is the father of lies.

The Gospel hasn't changed because God is the same yesterday, today, and forever. If anything has changed it is our perspective and interpretation of God's word. Skeptics will say the Bible can't tell us anything of any real value because everyone interprets it differently. We Christians, in fact, believe/disagree on many biblical things; however, one reason there are many different interpretations is because [speakers, pastors, evangelist, teachers, prophets, apostles] don't follow any sensible or consistent method of text exegesis. The inconsistencies then lead to inaccurate, inconsistent, illogical, and naïve interpretations amongst the Christian family.

I intend to go back to the meat of the Bible. The funny thing about the Word of God is that it simple of enough for a child to understand, yet deep enough for a Theologian to drown in. The problems usually occur when we attempt to get people to think we are smarter than we actually are. Studying God's precious book will be a lifelong experience. And if we are truly honest with ourselves we will admit that the more we dig into the Bible the less we actually know.

We find out why the Bible is called *The Living Word*. Jesus says that man should not live by bread alone, but by every word that proceedeth out of the mouth of God. That word proceedeth means that God is still speaking to us through his word. This is why when one is dealing with issues in his/her life and hears a sermon preached he/she feels the preacher is speaking directly to them. God's Word is so powerful and life changing that one scripture can heal any ill you may have. Jesus died that the world might live. And though he testifies that his coming will be quick, I say, *Even so, come, Lord Jesus, Come.*

HowardCarterMinistries@yahoo.com

CPSIA information can be obtained at www.ICGtesting.com
Printed in the USA
LVOW042249041111

253635LV00004B/96/P